DEFENDING THE BORDERS
THE TEXAS RANGERS,
1848-1861

John Salmon Ford. This picture of "Rip" Ford was probably taken in connection with the great raid on the Comanches in 1858. The high crown hat is typical of the period. While obviously a studio portrait, the gauntlets and leather coat have a used look, not the feel of studio props. The revolver belt and holsters are worn in a fashion shown on several other contemporary photographs.

Courtesy of Mr. John McWilliams, Stockton, California.

DEFENDING THE BORDERS
THE TEXAS RANGERS,
1848-1861

by

FREDERICK WILKINS

STATE HOUSE PRESS
Austin, Texas
2001

Library of Congress Cataloging-in-Publication Data

Wilkins, Frederick, 1916-
Defending the borders : The Texas Rangers,
1848-1861 / by Frederick Wilkins. ~1st ed.
p. cm.
Includes bibliographical references and index.
ISBN 1-880510-76-6 (alk. paper)
ISBN 1-880510-78-2 (deluxe ed. : alk. paper)
ISBN 1-880510-77-4 (pbk. : alk. paper)
1. Texas Rangers~History~19th century.
2. Texas Rangers~Biography
3. Texas~History~1846-1950
4. Texas~History, Military~19th Century
5. Frontier and pioneer life~Texas. I. Title

F391.W66 2001
976.4'05~dc 21   2001031373

Printed in the United States of America

FIRST EDITION

cover design by David Timmons

STATE HOUSE PRESS
PO Box 15247
Austin, Texas 78761

for

ORA LOU MCMAHAN WILKINS

TABLE OF CONTENTS

LIST OF ILLUSTRATIONS

PREFACE

T his, the third volume in a four-book history of the Texas Rangers in the Nineteenth Century, covers the largely neglected period between the close of the Mexican War and the opening of the Civil War. During these years from 1848 to 1861, Texas experienced a marked increase in population as thousands of people emigrated from the other states of the United States. Many resident Texans joined the immigrants, moving from the settled eastern counties to the west and developing a series of frontier settlements in country that had been unknown just a few years earlier. The Rio Grande region, following the Mexican War, saw a series of army posts established to protect what was now the southern border of the United States, and civilian settlements grew around each of these posts.

To the south, west and north, the advancing frontiers of Texas collided with Indian bands traveling south after horses and plunder as they had for generations. The United States inherited the war that the Texas Republic had been fighting with the Comanches for over a decade, and the old differences between the Texans and the Mexicans did not vanish when Texas joined the other states. The solutions to these problems seemed simple enough in Washington: the U.S. Army established a series of posts and sent garrisons to man them, and the federal government engaged in diplomatic negotiations with both Mexico and the Comanche chiefs.

Unfortunately, none of this really worked—at least not for any period of time. A love/hate relationship developed between the Texans and the U.S. Army, and Texas was soon forced to call upon its own defense forces to keep the Indians out of the frontier settlements. The state's answer was the formation of ranger companies, variously called Texas Rangers, Mounted Volunteers, Minute Men or Mounted Rangers. This book is the story of the years between wars when the Texas Rangers managed, but just barely, to defend the frontiers.

In telling this story, every effort has been made to find and use the primary source materials still available. Despite disastrous fires that burned many documents from the early years of this period, considerable numbers of the original muster rolls, correspondence, quartermaster papers and reports still exist in the archives of the State Library. Each of Texas' governors took a personal interest in the rangers, and the files of the governors' letters are a treasure trove for the ranger researcher. Unlike later periods when many of the individual rangers wrote of their services, only one man left any substantial record from the 1850s; John Salmon Ford's *Memoirs*, edited and published as *Rip Ford's Texas*, partially make up for this lapse.

Even though a substantial amount of material for reconstructing the period from 1848 to 1861 is available, little effort has been made to tell the ranger contribution to Texas during this difficult time; most extant histories recount only the few big events and omit the rest. In truth, on the surface it does appear that many ranger units were formed but that nothing of permanent value was accomplished. The Indian raids still continued.

Each governor fought the same problem: there was no money to keep the rangers in the field for any length of time. For the most part, by the time a company or detachment was settled in and functioning as a ranger command, its time of enlistment had expired. New dangers caused other units to be organized, with the same results. The answer, a permanent, large ranger force, was realized early.

Despite all the problems, the short-term ranger commands did provide some degree of protection to ever-expanding settlements and isolated farms. The testimonials from citizens residing within the defended areas show how much the Texans of the time thought of the rangers. Even though much of their hard and unglamorous work has been overlooked in the excitement of the Cortina trouble or by the major expeditions into Comanche territory, it was nevertheless the contribution of the rangers that allowed settlement to continue and expand. Defending the borders allowed Texas to grow.

Fortunately, the lessons from this decade were not ignored completely and led to the final establishment of a ranger force, in 1874, that was the culmination of all the difficult days and years that had begun in the 1820s.

So, after all the years of neglect, here are a few words of appreciation to the rangers of 1848-1861.

ACKNOWLEDGEMENTS

Once again, I thank Donaly Brice for his assistance in working with the extensive Texas Ranger records in the State Archives. In addition, he furnished me material on the Callahan Raid from his own collection. Over several years, members of the Archives Division photocopied documents and were always more than willing to answer questions by mail or telephone. It would have been impossible to write this book without their help.

John McWilliams generously provided the photo of John Salmon Ford. Additional photos were supplied by the Institute of Texan Cultures and the Library of the Daughters of the Republic, San Antonio. Weapon photos were furnished by the Texas Ranger Hall of Fame and Museum, Waco.

And my thanks to Trinity University, San Antonio, for permission to use its extensive collection of Texana material.

ROADS WEST

T he days following the Mexican War must have been a wonderful time for Texans. They had sent a considerable number of units to fight in Mexico, and the various regiments, battalions and individual companies had served in combat with distinction. The Texas units—universally labeled rangers—became nationally known, the first time the Texas Rangers had been recognized outside their own boundaries.[1] In addition to the ranger units fighting in Mexico, there were a considerable number of ranger companies protecting the Texas frontier, all financed by the United States. During the ten years of the Republic and the decade and a half of unofficial service during the colonial period, it was the only time ranger commands, by whatever name, had been paid on a regular basis. In historical honesty, this battlefield success was not always carried over into noncombat situations.

The war over, the U.S. government saw no reason to maintain hundreds of Texans under arms, and most of the ranger companies were disbanded. The often severe Indian raids that had plagued the Texas frontier had not been as much of a problem during the Mexican War. The army had fought a major campaign against the Seminole Indians in Florida in recent years, but none of the army's commanders had any idea of how to fight horse Indians. If they thought about Plains Indians at all, it was probably to dismiss the bow-and-arrow Comanches as backward savages. As rapidly as possible, the army moved units to defend the new frontier along the Rio Grande and began to survey and establish camps and forts across the unknown Texas frontier.

The Texans were naturally concerned with their own state, but the army had to consider Texas as just one part of vast new territories, annexed or conquered in the past three years, which required protection, and all areas were equally entitled to military forces. The law was clear enough, but there were just not enough troops to go around. When the peace treaty was signed, with land ceded or seized, there was much still unknown about the lands of New Mexico, California, Arizona and Nevada. For that matter, much of Texas was unexplored.

The discovery of gold in California in January 1848 added another incentive for the existing westward expansion. By 1849 it was common belief that gold could be discovered in every stream and mountainside in California and the great gold rush was on—even if most people had no clear idea of how to reach the Pacific. In addition to the desirability of opening routes to the gold fields, the government had other important requirements for new routes to the West Coast. Mail and passenger lines were needed, and army posts had to be located and then supplied. There had been steady trade between St. Louis and Santa Fe for many years, but this was as far west as any route which could be called a road had been developed. The Dragoons had laid out a trail from Santa Fe to the Pacific during the Mexican War, opening one route, but by 1848 a southern road was desperately needed so that emigrants from the southern states could reach the Pacific.

Unfortunately, few had any idea about the country south of the St. Louis-Santa Fe trail. An attempt to reach Santa Fe in 1842 had ended in disaster for a party of Texas traders. There had to be a route west from the Texas settlements—but where? San Antonio was the major western town on the southern frontier, and Castroville and a few settlements in the area were a half day further west, but beyond that was nothing. Fredericksburg was a small town, settled recently by German immigrants. The state capital, Austin, was seventy miles northeast of San Antonio. Dallas was far to the north, little more than a village. Along and in advance of this line, brave men and women were starting to farm. Each night they watched the sun vanish into an unknown west.

The army took the initiative in finding a new road to the Pacific through uncharted west Texas, but the army's initiatives were superseded by a civilian enterprise led by the most famous of the ex-rangers, Colonel John Coffee Hays.[2] "Jack" Hays had become famous during the Mexican War, and his fame evidently had much to do with his selection to head an expedition to find a wagon road to El Paso del Norte.[3] Hays talked an old friend, Samuel Maverick of San

Military Plaza, San Antonio Texas. From a contemporary engraving.

Antonio, into joining the expedition, a fortunate act for historians because Maverick maintained a brief journal.[4] His daily notations, with estimates of the distances traveled and the general direction of the march, are helpful in trying to retrace Hays' route. A new friend, John Caperton, also joined Hays and later wrote his account of the expedition as part of a biography of Hays.

This civilian-led enterprise was provided a ranger escort. On August 22, 1848, an order from Headquarters, Texas Mounted Volunteers, directed Captain Samuel Highsmith to accompany Hays and his party with one lieutenant, a corporal, bugler and thirty-four privates from his ranger company.[5] Highsmith was an experienced officer, having commanded a ranger company on the Texas frontier since 1846; he had recently mustered in a new company, and was stationed above Enchanted Rock on the Llano River.[6]

On August 27, 1848, Hays and the San Antonio contingent departed town, heading northwest for Fredericksburg.[7] They picked up the rangers with some Indian scouts at their camp on the Llano River and began the real part of the journey on September 5.

The first major barrier they encountered was a twisting river with steep banks which Hays called Devils River, the name it still bears. By this time it became clear that the maps and surveys they had were inaccurate, little more than guesses. It was also apparent the guide was not familiar with the region. They next reached the Pecos, which

made the Devils River seem like a placid stream. Just where and how
they crossed the canyon of the Pecos cannot be determined;
unknown to them, the river does not flow southward in a regular
course and, once across, the expedition had to find yet another crossing when they discovered the river had made a horseshoe bend and
again barred the way. By now, the country had changed dramatically
and they were in a semi-arid wasteland. Water was scarce; men and
animals suffered from heat and thirst.

After about a month on their trek with an estimated 418 miles
behind them, they had probably covered only about half that distance
in a direct line. They eventually traveled south and found the Rio
Grande, improving morale even if they were no better off than
before. Hays relieved the guide of his duties and took over the direction of the march, although he had no real idea where they were
going.[8] By October 4 the expedition's supplies were exhausted and
they subsisted by hunting and eating mustang meat.

Somehow the expedition managed to enter the Big Bend, keeping
alive by fortunate discoveries of water and game. The animals were
wearing down and the men were desperate, but by sheer chance they
ran into a party of Mescalero Apaches and, for once, both sides acted
with reason. Hays and his party gave the Apaches gifts, and the
Indians told them where to find a trail that led into Mexico and civilization. It seems likely this was the famous Comanche War Trail,
which led them across the Rio Grande to San Carlos in Mexico.[9]

The Texans reached the Mexican town and were well treated by
the surprised inhabitants. Here, and later in Presidio del Norte, Hays
was careful to explain they came as friends, not invaders. It must have
been evident the Americans were in no condition to fight; most were
barely alive. The Mexicans furnished them food and supplies and
gave them directions to Presidio, where they were again well treated.
Near this settlement on the Rio Grande they met Ben Leaton, one of
the first Americans in the region, who gave them shelter in the huge
adobe fort he was building and provided them with additional supplies.[10]

With food and rest, the expedition assumed some measure of its
early condition. Hays, while a long way from El Paso, decided not to
test the rest of the Big Bend; the way west would have to be found
by others. Part of his decision may have been based on Highsmith's

orders and the length of time the rangers could be away from their post on the frontier. On October 31 the column started northeast from Presidio del Norte.

The return trip, from Presidio to the Horsehead Crossing on the Pecos, is as much in dispute as most of the outward trip. Various accounts have them moving northeast, moving along mountains until they found a pass and turned east. If they forded the Pecos at the Horsehead Crossing, which is indicated, they evidently retraced part of the Comanche Trail. After crossing the Pecos they split their forces because Highsmith and his men arrived back at their camp on December 20, 1848. Highsmith arrived just in time, because the various ranger companies still on duty on the Texas frontier were being mustered out of federal service. Highsmith and his men marched south to Austin and were discharged on December 26, 1848,[11] the last of the Mexican War rangers to be on the United States' pay roll.

Hays and most of the civilians headed for San Antonio with a clearer idea of the terrain, even if they had not personally ridden over the region. Again the party split; most continued to Fredericksburg then to San Antonio, while Hays and a small party went south to explore the Las Moras Spring area near present day Bracketville. Hays and his detachment reached San Antonio on December 10, 1848, by which time everyone had given them up for lost.

Hays' report, and some early accounts of it, treated his expedition as a considerable achievement; his reputation was so great that anything he did was assumed to be successful.[12] Actually, the expedition was successful only in a negative way; Hays had showed where *not* to go. His rangers and civilians in his expedition were extremely fortunate to have returned alive. It was clear that the way to El Paso could not be reached easily by traveling up the Rio Grande, and it was equally certain the route did not lie through the Big Bend, which had been unknown until then. Also, something was now known about the lower Pecos River and the generally impassable gorge that swallowed the lower part of the river. Any road to the west would have to lie far to the north.

The attempt to find the way west was Hays' last service in Texas, his final association with the rangers. He took his family and some friends, Caperton among them, and went to live out his life in California.

Because of his fame, the expedition of Hays attracted considerable attention, and yet another party departed San Antonio a few months later but without much in the way of public notice. This expedition, much smaller, was also sent out because of the army's interest in finding suitable routes to El Paso. On February 26, 1849, Major General William Jenkins Worth, the Department Commander, ordered Robert S. Neighbors to find a suitable way west,[13] a choice probably made because Neighbors was the Supervising Indian Agent in Texas and had access to Indian guides. He selected several eastern Indians—Delaware, Shawnee and Choctaw—but the Indians and Jim Shaw, Neighbor's interpreter, remained worried about crossing Comanche lands in small numbers.

In a fortunate turn of events, Neighbors' effort to find additional men to reinforce his party resulted in the addition of John Salmon Ford, living in Austin. Ford had started in Texas as a doctor and was still generally addressed as Dr. Ford, but he had long since abandoned medical work, had worked as a newspaperman, and then had found his true calling as a ranger. In the Mexican War he had served as Hays' adjutant in Central Mexico. Unlike most staff officers, Ford spent his time fighting. It is likely he found peace boring and welcomed the opportunity to go campaigning again. He was as interested in recording events as leading a charge, and he later wrote extensive accounts of his life as a ranger.[14]

Because of his concern about the Indian reaction to an expedition's crossing their land, Neighbors and his party rode to one of the main Comanche camps. There was considerable opposition to having Buffalo Hump, one of the leaders, act as a guide, and Neighbors replaced him even though the Comanche had already been partially paid. The Texans and their Indian allies spent some time with the Comanches, recruited a new Comanche as guide, and finally started out in earnest about noon April 5.[15]

For whatever reason, probably because of their Comanche guide's familiarity with the region, they moved well north of the trail of the earlier expedition and thus avoided the difficulties that bedeviled Hays in trying to cross the lower Pecos. They forded the Pecos at the Horsehead Crossing and clearly traveled along part of the Comanche War Trail. Neighbors' report is quite brief. Ford had the advantage of time and space when he wrote his version of the expedition, but he does not have much detail that can be specifically related to the terrain they crossed. By avoiding the lower Big Bend and crossing easier terrain with more water, they did not experience the hardships of the earlier expedition. It was not a simple journey, however, and when they finally struck the Rio Grande they were sorely in need of supplies. Neighbors took one of the men and the best mules and rode ahead, hoping to find food for the others, leaving Ford to lead the remainder of the group. After a few days Ford's group was met by a Mexican carrying supplies for their relief, and all reached the settlement at San Elizario safely.

They rested before continuing on to El Paso del Norte and the settlement on the American side of the Rio Grande. Neighbors had seen that the route up the river was not suitable for an all weather road and found a guide to show them the way back to the Pecos along an old Mexican route. They returned by way of the Hueco Tanks, south of the Guadalupe Mountains, picking up streams that drained into the Pecos. Here their guide left them, and they rode down the Pecos and recrossed at the Horsehead Crossing.

The first beneficial result of the return trip took place near the crossing when they encountered a party of emigrants; one of the Texans signed on as a guide to lead the train to El Paso. As they reached the headlands of the Concho they found another group hopelessly lost and out of food. The dispirited travelers also obtained a guide to lead them to El Paso. Ford and Neighbors, backtracking their original route, found still another party at the old Spanish presidio on the San Saba River near present day Menard. For the third time, one of the expedition turned back to act as guide.[16] Neighbors and his party headed south for Fredericksburg and arrived in San Antonio early in June, because his report was written on June 4.[17]

It had not been an easy trip, and they made quite an impression as they rode though the streets of the little town. Ford recalled he wore a pair of drawers, a breech clout, a dirty shirt and no coat. One saloon and restaurant at first refused to serve him a drink.[18] There must have been considerable toasting of the successful conclusion of their expedition. After cleaning up and obtaining decent clothing, Ford worked with Neighbors on the official report and then returned to Austin.

Neighbors noted that they had not been issued instruments to make a regular topographical map of the new route and had been charged only with finding a trail that could be made into a wagon road without undue labor. They were satisfied this had been done. Unknown to Neighbors and Ford, an army survey party led by Lieutenants W.F. Smith and W.H.C. Whiting had arrived in San Antonio just a few days before, after opening another road to El Paso. This group had at least one person from the Hays' expedition as a guide and had moved westward from San Antonio to the Las Moras Springs then up to the Pecos. The rest of the way was much the same as Neighbors return trip.[19] Within a short time, Neighbors' trail became the Northern Road and the Whiting-Smith route the Southern Road. The army road was shorter and better for wagon trains leaving San Antonio; the North Road had advantages for travelers moving west through central Texas.

By mid-1849 it was clear wagon trains could cross Texas to El Paso del Norte. Travel became heavy, and the army began establishing posts out in territory that had been unknown even a year earlier. In this activity, two ex-rangers had played important roles. One had departed for California, but the sometime doctor, newspaperman and former ranger, Ford, was still in Texas. In closing his report, Neighbors told the new Department Commander, William S. Harney:

> In Dr. John S. Ford, I found an energetic and able assistant, the services performed by him were important to the successful termination of the expedition. I cheerfully recommend him to your favorable notice.[20]

The commendation did not go unnoticed.

THE RANGERS AND
THE U.S. ARMY

I t is doubtful if either Texas or the United States obtained exactly what they expected when the Republic entered the Union. The Texans hoped all their financial troubles would be over and that the United States would pay for Indian protection. Washington certainly never anticipated the extent of the Indian problem, but by 1849 both sides agreed that there *was* a problem.

The U.S. government considered the defense of any state to be the responsibility of the army. The Texans agreed only to a point; what they really wanted was to handle their own defense with the federal government's paying the bills. In such manner the love/hate relationship between Texas and the army developed.

The army made a gallant effort to defend the new state and the other new territories acquired by the war with Mexico. At the time, the U.S. Army had about ten-thousand men, and between a third to a fourth of this force was deployed in Texas in the years following the war. The number of company-sized units was impressive, but there was more than just the total number of companies to be considered. In 1849 there were only three mounted regiments in the army: the 1st and 2nd Dragoons and the Mounted Rifles. Although the government stationed a disproportionate number of horse-mounted companies in Texas, there were never enough to cover the vast territory open to Indian attack. The Texans complained that three-hundred horsemen could not patrol the exposed frontier of the Rio Grande and the Nueces.[1] The infantrymen did the best they could, riding in wagons to establish posts, then building quarters while patrolling on foot or muleback. It was not the answer, and newspaper editors often complained vociferously.[2]

Calling on state troops for help seemed the simple answer to the Texans. Many of the U.S. Army's senior commanders in Texas saw units such as the rangers as exterminators rather than as a police force to protect the Indians on the reservations; Brevet Major General George Brooke presented this view to the army in late summer 1849.[3] As the months went by, however, Brooke began to see the magnitude of the Indian menace. As Department Commander, he was authorized to call upon the governor for state troops for six months service, or at the pleasure of the president.[4] By the end of summer he was forced to ask for three ranger companies.[5]

As early as May, some communities had given up on official help and formed emergency minute men companies or detachments for local defense. During the night of May 14, 1849, an Indian raiding party rode along the San Antonio River above Goliad and stole every horse they found. A posse followed the trail the following day, finally losing the tracks and returning home. Two weeks later, another band hit the Mission Refugio, again riding along the San Antonio River, stealing or killing all the stock along the way. They entered one house, telling two slaves they were going to Goliad to whip the Americans. R.E. Sutton, a rancher, saw the Indians and sent a messenger to alert the townspeople in Goliad.

Faced with this threat, a volunteer company was formed with J.W. Johnson as captain. They found the trail of the raiders and followed the tracks through the night. Sutton, who reported the incident, said one of their horses followed the Indians—the Texans themselves could not make out the prints through the thick brush. When they caught up with the raiders, the Indians had stopped to rest, not suspecting they had been followed. Johnson was within a hundred yards when he formed his men into a line and charged.

The surprised Indians made no real effort to fight and scattered into the brush. A few managed to reach their horses and gallop off, but some were seen to fall from their horses as the Texans fired their rifles. Riding across the abandoned camp, the Texans found buffalo robes, shields, lances and blankets; the Indians had grabbed their bows and quivers and left everything else. Nine horses were recaptured, along with a large store of weapons and equipment. The minute men spent another night in the field under a pouring rain; by morning and clearing weather, all tracks were washed out and the volunteers returned home.

With two raids within a short period, the settlers along the San Antonio River sent Johnson to the governor with a petition requesting that a ranger company be established to patrol the country along the river. If they were not defended, the settlers said, they would have to abandon the area. Governor George T. Wood authorized Johnson to raise a company to protect the area along the San Antonio River below Goliad, and on July 7, 1849, a company was formed with Johnson as captain and Sutton as 1st lieutenant. They patrolled with considerable success, keeping Indians out of their area.

After they had been in service for two and a half months, the men heard about General Brooke's request for three ranger companies to be mustered into the U.S. service. They marched up to San Antonio to be mustered in, only to find that three commanders had already been selected. Sutton must have talked to the governor during this trip, because he reported later the volunteers returned to their station to serve out their time evidently with some implied promise that the governor would ask the legislature for funds to pay them for their time. Unfortunately, Captain Johnson was killed in an "affray." When a private was drowned trying to cross the San Antonio River and many of the volunteer rangers were sick, acting commander Sutton hoped the state would reward the company doctor for his untiring service.[6]

Whether the volunteers were ever paid is unknown; given the era in Texas, it seems unlikely, but the newly authorized companies did have the public interest. The *Texas State Gazette* reported that Ford, Gamble and Smock had command of the three new units.[7] This new command marked the official return of Ford to ranger service, a lucky day for the Texas frontier. The doctor-turned-soldier had commanded a volunteer unit chasing Indians in early 1849 and seemed a logical choice to lead one of the new companies. He was not, however, a favorite of Governor Wood, who had another candidate in mind, possibly Johnson though this is not certain. Wood deferred making a selection and left Austin for a time; in his absence the adjutant general, Colonel John D. Pitts, designated Ford as one of the commanders. Upon his return, Wood was unable to remove Ford, and the new ranger captain formed his unit on August 23, 1849.[8]

Ford's command was sent to the Nueces Strip, the region between the Rio Grande and the Nueces River which was, at the time, the most dangerous area in Texas. Largely unsettled, the region's wild horses brought in Mexican and American horse traders—and thieves. Seminole and Kickapoos rode north from Mexico looking for mounts, and the Comanches came south after horses, as they had for generations. There was considerable trade between San Antonio, Laredo, and the new settlements of Corpus Christi and Brownsville and across to Matamoros. Several forts established along the international boundary had little settlements growing around them. Brave people tried to establish new ranches or keep old properties operational. All this activity, plus the seemingly endless supply of wild horses, attracted every shade of criminal.

The new ranger company headed into this war zone, traveling by way of Corpus Christi to draw weapons and stores from the army depot there. Ford's command was a far cry from those during the Mexican War, or even from the days of the late Republic when many of the rangers had revolvers and all owned rifles. He mentioned that only a few men in his unit had revolvers and that "A dozen determined Indians could have defeated the whole command with heavy loss."[9]

Fortunately, they reached Corpus Christi without incident and were outfitted. Establishing his first camp some eight miles outside the town, Ford soon led most of his company on an extended scout after Indians. They rode through hard rains on the road from San Antonio to Laredo and down to Fort McIntosh at Laredo. After resting their tired mounts and resupplying, the rangers returned to their camp. Although they had seen no action, the men became familiar with the country and with some of the ranchers.[10]

During this period, Ford spent time drilling his company. He seems to have been alone in requiring practice of some form of drill and discipline, not the formal, rigid instruction of the army but a simple set of commands and formations suited to the high spirited Texans. He trained his men in a few basic formations—form column, form line, change directions—which were all necessary maneuvers for meeting a sudden Indian attack. He also required each man to take his turn at guard duty. If a ranger did not perform as required, the man could not go on scouts, act as an escort, or perform any other dangerous duty and was limited to guarding the camp and wagons or doing camp chores. Unit morale was high, but despite high spirits and constant patrolling Ford completed his first six months on February 23, 1850, with no significant Indian contact.[11] Not too much is known about the other two ranger companies. Ford had some contact and cooperated with Captain John Grumbles' company and mentioned it was stationed some seventy-five miles above Corpus Christi.[12]

One of the few documents from these three companies is a report of a scout by members of Grumbles' company. A Major Bryant was killed near Goliad by a raiding party, and the rangers heard about the murder the next evening. They left the following morning after the Indians had a long start, but the rangers kept after them, following a clear trail. It was almost impossible to run down a war party with such a lead, but the Texans persisted. They found worn out and lanced horses all along the trail, but the Indians had enough spare mounts to keep ahead of their pursuers. The rangers kept up the chase for six days, covering an estimated *three-hundred* miles! They regretfully gave up the chase and came back to camp.[13] What the third company accomplished is unknown.

Ford formed a new company the day following the mustering out of the original unit.[14] A considerable number of men reenlisted: Dr. Philip N. Luckett stayed on as surgeon; Andrew J. Walker, who had been a scout earlier, was elected 1st lieutenant; M.B. Highsmith became the 2nd lieutenant; David M. Level was orderly sergeant, the senior sergeant. The new guide was Roque Maugricio of Mexican-Indian parentage. He had lived with the Comanches and spoke their tongue; as a skilled tracker he was a valuable addition to the company. Ford moved and established a new camp on the river road between Laredo and Rio Grande City, about forty-five miles from Ringgold Barracks from where they could be resupplied.

Although the rangers could draw rations and usual supplies from their nearby army base, they had to go to Corpus Christi for weapons. Shortly after the company was reorganized, Ford had to march to Corpus Christi to replace their old army pistols. He decided to make an extensive scout on the way, going upriver to Fort McIntosh at Laredo for resupply then cutting across to Corpus. They marched expecting trouble, with Lieutenant Walker's commanding one part of the company and Ford the other. Sergeant Level, Maugricio and a few trusted rangers rode ahead, moving quietly, hoping Indians might see one group, turn away, and run into the other party. Walker's party did see Indians but lost them after a long chase.

The rangers broke camp the morning of May 12 and soon crossed the tracks of the same Indian party Walker had chased the day before.[15] Moving along the low ground, the rangers entered the Nueces Valley, following the tracks across the river. It was clear the Indians, riding leisurely through the woods, thought they had escaped when they outran Walker. The Texans could track them by the leaves on the prickly pears, slashed by Comanche whips.

The Comanches were legends in trailcraft and cunning, but they were also occasionally caught by surprise by the rangers. This day, Ford and his men followed them out of the woods and onto open prairie without the Indians' knowing they were anywhere near. When Ford began to gallop after them, shouting "Here they are!", most of the rangers unfortunately thought this was a command to remain in place. Ford, Level and Roque, the scout, found themselves chasing sixteen Comanches who were now aware they were being followed. The Indian chief saw his advantage and yelled they could easily kill three men. Secure in the advantage of numbers, the Comanches took a little time to get ready, just enough for the other rangers to realize what had happened and come galloping to help Ford and the others. By the time the Indians wheeled to fight, the numbers were nearly even.

In a close fight, the bows and arrows of the Comanches gave them a marked advantage. In this group of rangers, only Ford and Level had revolvers; most of the rangers were armed with issue Mississippi Rifles and single-shot muzzle-loading pistols. The rifle was accurate but was an infantry weapon, too long for easy use in the saddle. Once the rangers fired their single shot weapons, the Comanche warrior could fire a dozen arrows or rush in and use his lance before they could reload. Ford had trained his men in early ranger tactics, before the rangers obtained revolvers, in which the men were to stay together and fire in sequence, keeping some weapons loaded for close work while reloading as quickly as possible. Above all, they were never to be drawn out by Comanche tricks or taunts or feigned retreat.

The Comanche leader, as was customary, rode back to his men, encouraging them, then rode out to challenge the foe. When he insolently rode past Level, the sergeant shot at him, striking the chief in the arm. In the temporary confusion, Ford yelled for his men to charge. Giving the Texas yell, the rangers rushed in. The injured chief controlled his braves with a whistle, forming them in an "L" formation. Ford had instructed his men to maneuver to the right and rear of the Comanches, where it was most difficult for a bowman to shoot. Despite this, the Comanches twisted this way and that, shooting arrows up into the air. The falling shafts did some damage. Ford's horse was struck, and Ranger David Steele was hit by an arrow.

Ford crashed into one Comanche, throwing him to the ground where he was shot by another ranger. In one amazing incident, Doc Sullivan was challenged by one of the Comanches who asked if the ranger would kill a friend. The warrior evidently recognized Sullivan who, with Ford, had visited a Comanche camp on the way to El Paso in 1848. Old friends did not mean much to Doc Sullivan—he killed the Comanche.

The close quarter melee went against the Comanches and they scattered. The rangers chased them for four or five miles until the survivors were lost in dense woods. It was the first real fight for the company, and they could count four Comanche dead and another seven wounded. One body was left on the field, a sure sign of a demoralized and disgraced foe. They captured a dozen horses, bows, shields, lances and other abandoned equipment and personal gear. On May 29, the rangers captured a young Comanche boy who told them about the Indian losses. They returned to the Nueces and Comanche Crossing and placed a picket at the river. The Department Commander issued a general order praising the company, which must have made up for not capturing or killing the entire Comanche party.[16]

Because of his *Memoirs*, Ford's company is the best known ranger unit of this period. However, there were several other companies in service in early 1850. Besides the three companies called out by General Brooke, a newspaper story listed eight other officers leading ranger companies: Ben T. Hill, J.M. Smith, Jacob Roberts, John S. Sutton, Shapley P. Ross, Henry McCulloch, Isaac W. Johnson and Charles Blackwell. A later dispatch reported the Department Commander had asked the governor for a six-month company, and W.A. Wallace

"Big Foot" Wallace

had been appointed to command this unit.[17]

The story on Wallace's appointment was quite current, as he had been selected only three days before the news was in the paper.[18] Famous in Texas folk lore as "Big Foot," Wallace was well known, having been a ranger at times during the Republic. He fought at Salado Creek in 1842 and was on the expedition to the Rio Grande that ended in the fight at Mier. One of the unfortunate prisoners, Wallace fortunately escaped the black bean drawing and survived to return to Texas and fight another day.

In later years when he had assumed legendary status, he recounted a scout from his 1850 service. As he remembered, he had twenty rangers and was attached to Colonel Hardee, scouting along the Nueces River with orders to work on the west bank while the U.S. regulars covered the opposite side. The rangers rode almost to Corpus Christi, where they picked up a guide and fresh Indian tracks. They trailed the Indians, finding very fresh prints, the body of a Mexican, and army coats from Mexican and U.S. soldiers.

They eventually caught up with the Indians and engaged in a running fight with more than one band. Some of the fighting involved control of a water hole; the rangers were beginning to suffer from thirst. They finally watched the Indians ride away, carrying some dead and wounded. Wallace claimed twenty-two Indians were left on the ground, with another fifteen wounded. He killed many horses. His loss was three rangers wounded.[19] These figures seem quite high, based on other fights of the time and the numbers engaged; time may have enhanced Big Foot's memory. He remained on duty for his six months and was considered for an extension.[20]

Of the ranger companies supposed to have been in service at this time, Henry McCulloch is the only other commander who can be documented by surviving muster rolls, and these rolls are for late in 1850.[21] It seems likely McCulloch formed the third company called out in the summer of 1849, but he may have assumed command shortly after. Besides the mention of McCulloch as a ranger commander in a *Texas State Gazette* article on March 2, 1850, Ford mentions both captains John J. Grumbles and Henry E. McCulloch during this period and said McCulloch was operating between Goliad and Corpus Christi.[22]

There is a muster roll for a McCulloch-led unit in the Ranger Papers in the Texas State Library. It is doubtful that McCulloch continued to serve after his earlier 1849, or early 1850, enlistment was up, because one later account states this new company was formed November 5, 1850, in Austin, with the mission of protecting the country west of San Antonio.[23] The mustering-in location, Austin, of this unit is a considerable distance from his earlier patrol area, so a new unit after a break in service is indicated rather than a remustering of an old command.

McCulloch's report for December 1850 gives a view of typical ranger activities. McCulloch accompanied Lieutenant John R. King and ten men to visit Copano and assist King in his quartermaster duties. They checked the country along the bay to see if building a road was feasible. McCulloch examined the country along the bay and decided it was not fit for habitation.

When he returned to camp, McCulloch learned an Indian trail had been sighted. Satisfied with the number of sentries and patrols already out to follow the raiders, McCulloch sent King out to check the sentries. On his round, King had a brief skirmish with passing Indians and was slightly wounded.

McCulloch took what he could muster and started after these Indians. While he only managed to ride within sight of the fleeing raiders, he did keep them on the run. They finally abandoned their horses and fled on foot into the brush and escaped. McCulloch came back to camp with captured horses, blankets, lances, buffalo robes and other gear.[24]

This company served from November 5, 1850, until May 5, 1851. At this time, the unit was reorganized and transferred to Fort Martin

Scott near Fredericksburg. It served in the new area until November 4, 1851.[25]

McCulloch established his camp on the north fork of the Llano River and started patrolling. On one scout, with twenty-two men, McCulloch followed an Indian trail until he found the Indian camp. Once again the rangers achieved total surprise, and the braves were several hundred yards from their grazing horses when the rangers attacked. Four warriors in the camp were killed and the rest fled, leaving behind two squaws as prisoners.

The rangers returned to camp with the prisoners, treated them kindly and sent them back after a time, on good horses, with plenty of blankets. McCulloch explained they were not trying to kill Indians but were only trying to protect the settlements. If the Comanches would come in and make peace within the month, he would give them back all their captured property. A peace delegation did come to the post within the specified time, and the ranger returned their weapons and gear.[26] Just how long the truce lasted is unknown. The Comanches may have merely recovered some valuable property, but the incident reveals that Henry McCulloch was willing to try anything to accomplish his mission and protect the frontier.

McCulloch's muster rolls fill in some of the gaps in our knowledge of ranger units of 1850-1851. An interesting example is the strict accounting for supplies and equipment; if a ranger lost *anything,* it came out of his pay. The notations about a lost pistol, $7.50, or a lost rifle, $13.50, suggest these companies, like Ford's, were basically using army-issued, single-shot weapons. However, the rolls are filled with stoppages for 20-cent mainsprings, 34-cent waistbelts, 50-cent ramrods, and 45-cent upper bands. The excessive mention of weapon parts suggests either that their weapons were old stock or that the rangers were unusually hard on their arms. In his first company, McCulloch had mustered eighty-eight men; the second unit contained a total of eighty-nine. There was no automatic reenlistment; many rangers had enough after one period of service and went home. Fortunately, enough stayed to provide a good cadre for rebuilding a new command. Surprisingly few officers, sergeants or corporals reenlisted. Each unit had a bugler, a hospital steward, and farriers or blacksmiths.

Neither company showed any combat losses, but there were several deaths from illness and one discharge for health reasons. It was an exciting life, but harsh; "romantic" is a term that has been applied to the frontier only recently. McCulloch had one man discharged for drunken conduct. Again, it is easy to imagine the old rangers as devil-may-care, hell-raising types, but the reality was that a commander could not depend on drunks and they received quick discharges.

Several times expenditures are noted on the rolls showing corn was a regular item of issue. During the Republic and the Mexican War, it was mandatory for a ranger to have the best mount possible, and they grain-fed their mounts whenever possible. Documentation of this period does not discuss the care of ranger mounts as much as earlier, but there is no doubt obtaining and maintaining a good horse was a matter of high priority.

During this period the U.S. Army was facing new conditions and new problems just as the rangers were. In fact, some army officers considered the rangers to *be* the problem! Soldiers were expected to be peace officers even though their mission was to fight wars. They had to contend with hostile Indians, Mexican smugglers and bandits, American smugglers and outlaws, and even had to catch runaway slaves. This environment colored their feelings towards the Texans, especially the rangers. On November 24, 1849, the senior officer at Fort Brown, Colonel H. Wilson, wrote the Department Commander he had been informed a party of Texas Rangers and other men had crossed the Rio Grande near Roma and attacked a party of Mexican soldiers who had earlier seized some smuggled goods. The Texans had taken all the goods, plus the clothing, arms and equipment of the Mexican soldiers, and returned to Texas.[27]

Wilson had served with rangers during the late war; the relationship had not been friendly, and it is understandable that he would associate the rangers with outlaw behavior. A more balanced view was sent to headquarters by P.W. Humphreys a few days after Wilson reported. In his letter, Humphreys carefully outlined the situation along the Rio Grande. Much of the trouble was caused by excessive import duties which made smuggling a very profitable business. While there were official fees set by the Mexican government, the country was so disorganized that local custom officials often bid on admitting goods. In one case in which Camargo officials had levied a 25 percent duty, the smugglers merely traveled to Mier where they received a better rate!

Irate over the loss of duty, Camargo officials obtained a detachment of men, from the Mexican army, which went down to Mier and captured the goods. Somewhere along the road on their return to Camargo, an unidentified party from Texas crossed the river and captured everything: soldiers, customs agents, mules, goods, arms and equipment. They took everything back into Texas, where it was rumored they were paid two-thousand dollars for their trouble. Humphreys reported the incident but stressed there was no bloodshed.

Humphreys admitted that a considerable number of adventurers infested the region, attracted by excitement and making a good living by smuggling and pillaging. Some of their depredations were attributed to the Indians. Mexican mustangers made life difficult, and even impossible in certain areas. While he was in the region, Humphreys reported a "Mexican" living in Laredo had been murdered and that a farmer named Dawson had been robbed and killed by Mexican bandits. For the record, Humphreys heard that some of these criminals had been captured by rangers. Large parties of Mexicans roamed the Nueces Strip, supposedly hunting wild horses but actually picking up whatever crossed their path. It was dangerous for a convoy to travel the region unless heavily guarded.[28]

General Brooke was placed in an awkward position by Wilson's letter. It is to his credit that he did not automatically assume that rangers had been involved in the border crossing. Humphrey's report may have also given him a better perspective of conditions along the Rio Grande. He was, however, aware of the consequences if rangers *had* been involved, and he felt the matter required discussion with the governor.

> It is suggested in Col. Wilson's letter to Major Lamotte, that the party which crossed the Rio Grande belonged to the Rangers now in the service of the United States. This I cannot believe for a moment, and hope most sincerely that no officer attached to this Corps, can have so far forgotten his orders and duties as to have committed an offense which might

embroil the two countries in the most serious difficulties.

Brooke went on to express the likely result of any future ranger involvement in cross-river expeditions.

> Should the invasion have been made by the Rangers in service, it will lead no doubt to the instant disbandment of these troops, and to great objections thereafter to their employment.[29]

Governor Peter H. Bell and Brooke had a fine working relationship. In fairness, it must be noted that the Department Commanders did the best they could to support the state. Much of the difficulty and ill will that developed was due to a hesitant Texas legislature and its lack of funds. Bell realized this and did what he could to remedy an almost impossible situation. The state faced a multitude of problems, but a pre-eminent problem was its defense against attacks, from across the border, which cost lives and property and threatened frontier expansion.

On January 18, 1850, Bell sent a petition and a message to the legislature, outlining this situation. Talking about frontier defense, he said, "There is no subject more intrinsically important, and none more calculated to elicit from the representatives of the People, prompt, practical and judicious action." As governor, he had the authority to call emergency companies into service, but he had no authority to pay such units. Bell explained that he had before him many calls for help on the exposed frontiers. He asked the Honorable Legislature to indicate in what manner and by what means the absolute wants of these citizens could be met, then he concluded his appeal.

> I therefore respectfully recommend to the Legislature the passage of a law authorizing the Executive, when it may be deemed absolutely expedient, to call into service a competent force, defining, more definitely, his duties and powers.[30]

Governor P.H. Bell

This was the first of numerous attempts to persuade the legislature to define the powers of the governor, by law, so that he could raise and support ranger commands. Bell had no luck—nor did his successors—so he tried another route by appealing to the Congress of the United States. In a long resolution to Congress, Bell outlined the Indian problem as it applied to Texas. He pointed out the satisfactory and successful defense of the frontiers during 1847, 1848 and part of 1849 when state forces, paid and acting as U.S. troops, held the frontiers and controlled Indian raiding. He outlined the vast distances involved and the considerable funds required to meet the challenge. Since there was no state money available, he requested help from the federal government. Knowing the situation and aware of how many infantry companies had been assigned, he specifically asked for mounted troops.[31] The route attempted by Bell—for Texas to furnish rangers to be paid by the United States—would be traveled by his successors, but like Bell they would also become lost on the way.

Whether or not the criticism of the U.S. Army over not controlling the Indians was justified did not mean the senior U.S. commanders in Texas did not understand the problem. General Brooke had a very clear appreciation of what faced him and the Texans. In a letter to General Winfield Scott in early 1850, the Department Commander patiently explained it was impossible to make the Indians understand they could never win a war with the United States. They had no concept of either their own insignificant numbers or the overwhelming power of the Americans. Unfortunately, the weakness of the army forces available would never convince them of the imbalance in forces. A considerable increase in the number of army posts and depots would be necessary, while maintaining the established forts. Brooke emphasized that the predatory war then going on could last forever unless enough force was applied to end the raiding at once. Brooke outlined a concise plan to stop raids into Mexico by Comanche bands and protect the Rio Grande frontier: the Plains Indians must give up their horses, settle, and become agriculturists, with generous government annuities, or be exterminated![32]

A copy of the letter to General in Chief Scott was furnished Governor Bell, who agreed with most of the recommendations and comments of the Department Commander. In Bell's reply he placed considerable blame for the sad state of affairs on the nation's capital city, but he was honest enough to admit his own legislature was also at fault for not providing the means for Indian defense.

Bell did not censure the general; instead, he thanked him and praised him for the measures he had taken to defend the settlements. He said he had a lively sympathy for the Indians, who were in many ways innocent victims of conditions they neither wanted nor could control. Although historians a century and more later could afford to see the matter differently, the governor was forced to face conditions as he saw them and arrived at his solution.

> Your suggestions, General, are good; Let the Indians have a Country - hunting ground, trading houses to be established amonst them, - honest men to deal with and the trade properly regulated, and let annuities be given them. They should, if possible, be removed from all proximity to the settlements of this country. Too much blood has been spilled on both sides to permit us to be good neighbors. Indeed, I am satisfied that there is no other alternative than their removal, or their total destruction.[33]

Nothing came of these exchanges between the governor and the Department Commander, or with any of the officials in Washington.

At the highest levels of government there would be a growing consensus that the Indian troubles in Texas were exaggerated, with Texans responsible for much of the mischief. Along the frontier, it is doubtful if anyone knew or cared about the exchange of ideas and plans. The rangers were interested in good horses, some food and weapons and ammunition. Settlers and rangers alike were concerned about staying alive rather than diplomacy.

Some rough idea of the problem of staying alive in a ranger company of 1850 can be obtained by again following the adventures of Ford and his men. Of the companies formed in 1849 and the following months, only his unit can be examined in some detail.

After his defeat of the Comanche party on May 12, 1850, Ford had a continuing series of engagements with Indian raiders. The braves he had fought were a small part of a large band. The day after the fight, the rangers found that two horses had been picked up by Indians, and when Roque backtracked the trail he found that nine Indians had been involved.[34] Ford must have lost his horse because he had to borrow another mount to lead the chase after the stolen horses. It was bad enough when the Comanches stole horses from settlers, but losing their own animals was a blow to ranger pride! At times they came within view of the running Indians but not close enough for a fight. About sundown, they began to check their location and discovered they had been running in a huge circle and were about a mile from where they had started that morning.

The disgusted rangers walked their exhausted mounts to their new camp and established heavy security. It was a wise precaution because, with morning, they discovered a large Comanche band close by. Later, the Texans learned the Comanches who had survived the earlier fight had joined about seventy-five other warriors and turned back to find the rangers. They had turned away from the guards at the crossing on the Nueces and watched the chase after the nine Indians and the stolen horses. It had puzzled them, as they could not determine where the main body was camped. The two bands joined and circled the ranger camp, trying to cut off individuals or small groups or to lure the rangers out onto the open prairie.

Ford kept his men under strict control, not sending out hunters for fear of ambush. Ranger rations were low, and he decided to march to Fort Merrill and resupply. They reached the army post without trouble and drew rations and needed supplies. Ford reported he was riding a mustang pony and could not find a decent horse in Corpus Christi. They returned to their camp and, about three in the morning on May 26, the Comanches made a strong feint at the ranger position. Their attack, more an attempt to stampede the horses rather than an all-out assault, achieved limited success. The horse guards fired at the attackers but lost some animals. One Comanche managed to reach the center of the camp, yelling a request not to be shot, but the rangers could not understand him and shot him from his horse. Roque came and asked the dying man his name. The Comanche told them there was a large band near them, which came as no surprise. The dead warrior's horse, lance, bow and shield were slight repayment for the ranger loss.

As soon as there was enough daylight to see, the angry Texans started in unsuccessful pursuit; as they often did, the Comanches simply scattered in every direction to reassemble at some known point. It was stupid to waste the entire company chasing one or two Indians, and Ford sent a messenger to Captain J.B. Plummer, commanding Fort Merrill, telling him of the large Comanche band. The message was received with some doubt; most army officers never saw any Indians and believed the Texans were constantly crying wolf, trying to raise more troops or obtain funds.

Ford was joined by a detachment that had gone to the fort to exchange pistols. The entire company started back and resumed the search for the Indians on May 29. By now, for a variety of causes, most of the rangers were riding mustang horses. They made a late start because the mounts had to finish grazing before they could start.

About ten in the morning, they discovered a fresh trail and the rangers closed up, followed by a strong rear guard. Roque and two other rangers were well ahead as scouts. Several miles later, the scouts sighted a large Comanche party resting in a thicket of mesquite trees. Seeing the approaching rangers, the Indians gathered their gear and hastily mounted and started running. The company spread out, so they could use their rifles, and began chasing the Indians. Their Mississippi Rifles were an accurate arm, even though awkward to fire at the gallop, and several Comanches were seen falling to the ground. The rangers galloped over them without halting.

Ranger William Gillespie, one of the few men with a revolver, was riding behind Ford when an Indian fell from his horse, apparently dead or badly wounded. As Gillespie rode by, the supposedly dead man jumped up and bent his bow. The ranger snapped a shot, but Gillespie's horse shied and the ball struck the ground. The arrow struck Gillespie in the side. Two rangers rode up and helped him from his horse and into the shelter of some nearby trees.

Still leading the chase, Ford noticed a change in the Comanches ahead, which he believed might be a change of direction to strike the smaller rearguard. He yelled for his men to follow and saw they had stopped well back of him. For a bitter moment he thought they had lost their nerve. At this time, Roque rode up and told him Gillespie had been hurt and that the Indians seemed to be trying to go back and scalp him. Ford sent some of his men to protect Gillespie while maintaining pressure on the Comanches.

The rangers began a careful, long-range rifle fire that killed and wounded horse after horse in the Comanche band. Now and then, they struck a rider. The Comanches, afraid to charge against the deliberate rifle fire, were pressed back towards the ranger rear guard. It was not the way the Indians liked to fight, and they tried their old tactic of attempting to split the rangers by sending out two riders to draw out pursuit. One of his men started in pursuit, but Ford called him back and the ranger's horse fell, throwing the man into a pool of muddy water. He watched in disgust as his fellow rangers rode by, laughing at his predicament.

At this point, the rear guard rode up and hit the Comanches from the flank. It had been a somewhat even fight until then. Now the rangers had a slight advantage in numbers, and the Comanches seldom fought under these conditions. They began trying to save their dead and wounded, and Ranger Robert Adams had a brief hand-to-hand fight with one brave. One of the chiefs and a young brave gave their horses to dismounted wounded. The mounted Comanches tried sudden rushes at the approaching rangers, trying to slow them or draw them away from the Comanches running on foot for the shelter of the woods. Ford and Ranger David Steele ran after the chief, who had found another horse. Ford fired a revolver at over a hundred yards and hit the chief in the arm. He yelled for Steele to dismount and use his rifle. Ford grabbed the reins while Steele steadied himself and fired off a round, striking the Indian in the head.

Hearing firing to the rear, the rangers broke off the chase and rode back, resting their tired horses. They discovered the shooting was from a brief affray when a young warrior had been cut off and wounded several times. Roque rode into the woods where the injured Comanche was hiding and spoke to him in his tongue, promising him he would not be killed. To their surprise, the boy surrendered, informing them his name was Carne Muerto—Dead Meat!

Sergeant Level had also been wounded in the fight by a Comanche with a fine Swiss Yager, an accurate rifled hunting arm. The warrior caused considerable scampering for cover whenever he aimed the rifle at the rangers. Level had been hit by a ball that passed through his horse's shoulder and penetrated the ranger's leg.

The Indians were believed to have lost four dead and seven wounded, but it was hard to obtain an accurate count in such a running fight. The Comanches had carried off all bodies except the chief and the young prisoner. The band had been scattered, losing many horses, but the victory was bitter—young Gillespie died despite everything that could be done. He was carried to a nearby camp where part of Grumble's company was on duty. He died some eight hours after being hit. Members from both ranger companies formed an honor guard and fired a salute over Gillespie's grave.

The young ranger was part of a family that had served Texas from early days. He was a cousin of Captain R.A. Gillespie, a ranger of the Republic and a company commander in the Mexican War. Both cousins were unlucky; R.A. Gillespie was killed leading a charge in the battle for Monterrey.

After the funeral, the rangers rode back to their main camp, taking the prisoner with them. To their surprise, he made a remarkable recovery. When he learned the details of the second fight, General Brooke had his adjutant general send Ford another letter of commendation. In this message, Level, Adams and Gillespie were mentioned by name.[35]

Defending the frontier was not always a matter of chasing fleeing Indians and receiving complimentary letters. It was sometimes a matter of defeat and death. After the May victories, three members of Ford's company went home on leave to be witnesses in a legal dispute. They completed their court obligation and started back to camp. Alpheus D. Neal, Doc Sullivan and John Wilbarger were experienced rangers; Ford had cautioned them about traveling in small numbers in the Nueces Strip, but the men had overstayed their leave and were eager to return to duty. They rode by way of San Patricio, a small settlement, and stopped for a noon break near the present day King Ranch. The country was open prairie, with few trees.

As they were preparing to resume their trip, with their horses still tied up for the noon halt, they saw a large party of Indians within rifle range. For some reason the rangers decided to fight rather than run. The first shot from one of Comanches with a rifle hit Sullivan in the body, and the other rangers eased the badly wounded man to the ground. Sullivan sensed he was dying and motioned the others to run. A second shot struck him in the head, killing him. Wilbarger was either able to mount his horse again, or he was only able to grab his weapons and start running; much later when his body was found, blood clots on the ground indicated he had not died cheaply.

Neal managed to mount his horse again, but the startled animal bolted and ran under the rope Sullivan had used to secure his mount. He was jerked from the saddle, and the excited horse ran directly into the Comanches and was captured. Despite being an experienced ranger, Neal had tied all his weapons to the pommel before sitting down to eat lunch! Now, on foot and unarmed, all Neal could do was start walking towards the far distant camp of the rangers. The Comanches rode beside him, firing at him from time to time with his own rifle and pistol. He was hit repeatedly and finally fainted from loss of blood and pain.

The ranger collapsed near a shallow water hole. When he regained consciousness, he neither opened his eyes nor moved. For a time he heard Indians talking, and once he was certain someone approached to watch him. For some reason, the Comanches had not scalped him or mutilated his body. Finally certain they were gone, Neal managed to sit up and pulled or broke several arrows from his body and legs. He was on foot, naked, bleeding and weak from loss of blood, but he managed to walk and crawl sixty-five miles back to San Patricio!

After Neal told his companions what had happened, search parties found the bodies of Wilbarger and Sullivan. It appeared that the same Comanche band had been involved in this fight because

Sullivan's body had been terribly mutilated and the corpse dragged over the prairie; someone in the Indian party had recognized him from his stay in their camp. Part of the bloody Texas frontier saga, the fathers of Wilbarger and Sullivan had also been killed by Indians.[36]

Rip Ford was on the way to becoming a Texas legend, but it is fitting to note the captain was supported by some excellent lieutenants. In early June 1850, Comanches began raiding near Laredo, and Ford sent a detachment under Lieutenant Andy Walker to provide some protection to the area. Walker had been a scout and was elected a lieutenant when Ford's company was mustered in for a second enlistment. Taking twenty men, he established a camp near Laredo from where he could obtain intelligence from any of the people who had not fled their ranches.

In mid June he received news of a raid and started down river after the Comanches. The rangers caught sight of the Indians near one of the river ranches and took a position to block the intruders on their return, meanwhile unsaddling and resting their horses. The often unpredictable Comanches turned back sooner than expected, driving a large herd of captured horses towards the ranch corral. Many of the Indians were riding worn out horses, exhausted from the long march from the Plains, and they were herding the captured mounts into the corral to select fresh horses.

The dismounted rangers opened long range fire on the advancing Indians then ran for their horses. The Indians, few in number, started running. A chase of over a mile brought the lead rangers up with the Comanches. Rangers Ed Stevens and José Morales caught up to two braves, but one of the Comanches twisted about to shoot Stevens in the head with an arrow. The arrow point struck just below the hair line and cut across the ranger's skull. Stevens rode up beside the Indian and jammed his rifle muzzle against the man's temple and blew out his brains.

Morales knocked his prey from the saddle and wheeled about just as the Indian was trying to hit Stevens with an arrow. Morales ran the man down then knocked him down again and again before tiring of the game and shooting the Comanche. He rode over to help Stevens loosen the arrow from his scalp and bandaged the wound with his handkerchief.

The rest of the detachment galloped up, picking up the chase. In this second run, Stevens brought down two more warriors and Morales one. For once, the Comanches were on winded horses; seven of the eight warriors in the band were all killed and one badly wounded. The wounded Comanche was captured and taken back to a nearby ranch. He had both hips shattered, as well as other injuries; it was clear he would soon die. The rangers agreed it would be an act of mercy to shoot the poor man. Even though they had worked hard to kill him a short time earlier, none of them could shoot him under these circumstances. Finally, one of the ranch hands volunteered and killed the Comanche.

Ford reported all the stolen horses were recovered, but the greatest gain was the restored confidence of the Mexican ranchers and settlers in the area.[37] He decided to increase the force near Laredo and went to join Walker with a strong detachment. They took Carne Muerte, the young Comanche prisoner, to turn him over to the army at Fort McIntosh in Laredo. The Comanche was very friendly and willingly told them of other Comanche bands in the region. Ford left behind twenty-six men and a lieutenant to guard their permanent camp with strict instructions they were not to send out small patrols unless absolutely necessary. Once again, Ford sent word of Comanches in the area to the commander at McIntosh.

After the ranger detachment with Ford reached Laredo, there were rumors that the ranger camp had been attacked and overrun. The entire ranger force started back, accompanied by troops from the 1st Infantry. To their relief, the rumors were only partially true. The camp had been threatened for two days by a large Comanche band, but when the Indians had not been able to draw out or split the fortified rangers, they stole a few horses and scattered.

For some time after, the area was quiet. The bloody fights and the constant ranger patrols discouraged Indian raids, and there was a return to some semblance of peace. When this six-month term was up, Ford's company was reformed for another six-month enlistment on September 24, 1850.[38] Most of the men signed on again. A major change was the replacement of Lieutenant Highsmith by Ed Burleson, the son of Edward Burleson who had been one of the noted ranger commanders during the days of the Texas Republic.

Young Burleson would continue the tradition.

There had been considerable negotiations about the return of the prisoner, Carne Muerte, after it was learned he was the son of one of the Comanche chiefs who wanted him back. The government believed a peace treaty might be worked out based on his safe return. Everything possible had been done to make him happy, including visits by members of his family. In January 1851, Ford was instructed to send the young man to San Antonio. Lieutenant Ed Burleson and twenty men escorted the Comanche north, traveling by way of Fort Merrill.[39]

Ford was sick for most of the month, recovering in Laredo, and turned over the patrolling to his officers. However, when a Mexican was killed only two miles outside town, he led an unsuccessful scout after the marauders.

Once again, Andy Walker found action when the rangers discovered a clear trail leading into Mexico and a considerable number of hobbled horses and mules about fifty miles north east of Laredo in a ravine known locally as Arroyo Gato. The lieutenant suspected the herd had been left by Comanche raiders, who would not leave such a valuable group of animals alone for long. The Comanches would return with what they had found in Mexico and ride back to their main camps up on the Plains. Walker had his men hide any sign of their tracks and set up a hidden camp about two miles away.

Then the rangers waited...and waited...

Walker had sentries out two miles, with a picket midway between the scouts and his camp. The impatient rangers hid for six days! Towards four o'clock one afternoon, the scouts signaled the Comanches were returning. Seventeen Comanches were driving 150 mules and perhaps fifty horses, and the ranger scouts allowed them to ride by unmolested. The Indians were so busy herding the animals they never saw the Texans.

Meantime, Walker had mounted his detachment and charged the head of the column, the rangers yelling and firing. Caught by surprise, the lead Comanches were driven back into the herd. The band chief used a whistle to rally and signal his braves but was killed. Another warrior found the whistle and started signaling.

The fight was at close range with Indians, rangers, horses and mules in a confused tangle. The Texans split, trying to follow the scattered Comanches. Three Indians attacked Sergeant Level, who hastily dismounted and used his horse as a shield. While holding onto the pommel trying to steady his mount, an arrow struck his hand and literally nailed him to the saddle. Several more arrows killed the horse just as a Comanche charged the temporarily helpless ranger. Level yelled for help, and another ranger saw what was happening and shot the Indian.

Walker was also separated from the main group and was charged by several braves. He shot one from the saddle only to have the Comanche get up and charge him on foot. A second round killed the Indian. Wallace McNeill killed a warrior and captured his horse and gear. Ranger Volney Rountree threw himself to one side, when he saw a Comanche drawing his bow, but broke a stirrup strap and fell to the ground. The horse galloped off with Rountree's weapons. The ranger ran after the animal and jumped on a mule in an attempt to capture his horse. As he passed a dead Indian, the "corpse" jumped up and shot several arrows at him! Rountree was so startled he fell to the ground again and watched in disgust as the Comanche climbed on the mule and rode away.

Despite these individual skirmishes, the charge of the rangers had split the Comanches, killing four and wounding six or seven. The survivors scattered, either on foot or horse, and escaped. In their rush, they abandoned all the stolen animals and a Mexican boy captured in Mexico. He was very excited and kept praising the rangers; in time, they were able to return him to his family.

It was not a one sided victory—the Texans had one ranger killed and another wounded. They rounded up the stolen animals, and Walker turned them over to the quartermaster at Fort McIntosh. Most of the animals were restored to Mexican owners. There is a final note to the story when, later, a lawyer called on Ford and inquired about the animals the rangers had recaptured. He had been instructed to institute a suit for seven mules, claiming his client had lost thirty-five mules but only twenty-eight had been returned. Ford told him, none too kindly, that Walker had turned in all the animals recovered. Ford suggested the client was lucky to have recovered *any* mules. He mentioned that, had he been Walker, he would have cut off the ears of anyone who suggested such a suit!

There is no record of a lawsuit.[40]

January 27, 1851, two days after Walker's fight, Lieutenant Ed Burleson, was involved in a bloody skirmish on the San Antonio to Laredo Road. As mentioned earlier, he and a group of rangers had escorted Carne Muerte to San Antonio. On their return, Burleson saw three mounted Indians near the Nueces River crossing. It was fairly open country, and the ranger saw no reason to suspect an ambush. He called to eight of his detachment and started after the Comanches, instructing the others to keep to the road.

After a chase of several miles, the three Comanches rode up to eleven Indians on foot and turned to fight. Burleson spread his men and rode to within fifty yards and opened fire. He yelled instructions, but the sound of the shots muffled his commands and the rangers thought he had said to dismount. They did, using their horses as shields, and the Texans' advantage of mobility was lost. The Comanches saw their opportunity and rushed forward, shooting arrows on the run.

In the space of a moment, the air was full of descending shafts. The rangers used their mounts as best they could, firing under the bellies at the Comanches, now charging from the sides as well as the front. The fight was hand to hand, intense, brutal and quick. Ranger Baker Barton was struck by three arrows, all of them fatal shafts, and died standing up, holding his saddle pommel and firing his revolver. William Lackey was also hit three times. James Carr was struck several times. He was using a Colt carbine and seemed to have an arrow hit him every time he aimed the weapon. One shaft struck his finger as he was firing, splintering the stock. Carr shot a running Comanche who kept on for several steps, still using his bow, before he fell dead before the injured ranger.

Lieutenant Burleson was hit in the head with an arrow before he could kill his opponent. Alf Tom was wounded, as was Jim Wilkinson. The detachment guide, Warren Lyons, who had lived with the Comanches and spoke their tongue, yelled out translations of the orders of the band's chief to Burleson. Other than his clothing and arms, Lyons could have been a Comanche, running, jumping in the air, constantly changing direction and firing from all positions and angles.

Jack Spence was attacked by several Comanches; wounded, he yelled for help. The odds had shifted somewhat and there were several rangers not engaged. They rushed to his help, and the Indians turned and ran. Lyons listened to the surviving Comanches and told the rangers the fight was over and they had the field. The Comanches left four dead on the bloody ground; the rangers believed there were another eight wounded.

The rest of the detachment rode up just as the fight was ending. Burleson sent one of the rangers to a water hole some twenty miles distant, as they were out of water, and did what could be done for the wounded, sending a messenger to Fort McIntosh to bring wagons and medical help. They tied poor Barton on a mule and buried him a mile away, in case the Comanches returned later and found a fresh grave.

Close by, the rangers found a number of carts that had been on their way to San Antonio. The dismounted Comanches had been waiting to ambush the train when Burleson chased the three on horseback into the ambush site. The Mexican cart drivers were grateful and went their way. The injured rangers were transported to the army post in Laredo.[41]

Ford's company was mustered out and in again on March 21, 1851.[42] He had another fight which resulted in the capture of a herd of Comanche ponies but no casualties. Burleson chased another band for twenty miles, but it escaped into Mexico before the rangers could do any damage.[43]

Late in August, Ford and some of his men scouted for Indians who had been in a fight with Mexican troops. It was reported the Indians had crossed into Texas, but the rangers could never find a fresh trail. Conversations with Mexican forces suggested the raiders were Seminole, as they wore some clothing and were armed with rifles.[44]

The suspicions about the Indians were probably correct. Several months earlier, the Special Agent for Indian Affairs had warned Governor Bell that a notorious Seminole Chief known to the Texans as Wild Cat was negotiating with Mexican officials to bring his people to live south of the Rio Grande. He had already sent many Seminoles into Mexico, and others would follow as soon as the corn crop was in. Wild Cat was pressuring all the settled tribes to join him, even some of the Comanches.[45]

This letter followed a message from Marcus Duval, the Seminole Sub Agent, who warned that the Seminoles were planning to set up their own country just north of the Rio Grande. In addition to moving his own people, Wild Cat had escorted sizable numbers of escaped slaves into Mexico. Duval was worried that many smaller groups were hiding on the frontier, waiting the chance to flee into Mexico. Although he believed most of the blacks belonged to the Seminoles, there were some who had white owners.[46]

The governor evidently sent this information to General Brooke, who wrote back that the commander at Fort Duncan had informed him the Seminoles had not settled in Texas but over in Mexico. Authorities there had agreed to the Indian settlement, providing the Seminoles helped fight the Comanches, which they had done.

Brooke then mentioned the matter of slaves, a topic that would grow in importance and difficulty over the years. The general knew the Seminoles had many black slaves, and there was no easy way to determine ownership of such slaves. He had instructed army officers along the Rio Grande to hold any suspected slaves until definite proof of ownership could be determined. It was a delicate matter, a new and unwelcome responsibility for the U.S. Army.

> It is unusual to employ the Army, or any volunteers in the service, to arrest such persons; and as far as my experience goes, I do not recollect a single instance where such a course has been pursued.

In addition, Brooke informed the governor he had need for McCulloch's company where it was stationed and that Agent Rollins was going to San Saba for a peace conference.[47]

There were five volunteer ranger companies in service in early 1851, most of which were due for discharge in March. General Brooke wrote Governor Bell that he had a continuing need for the Texas volunteers and planned to call on the state for four complete companies, unless he received army reinforcements.[48] When no U.S. Army regulars were sent to Texas, the rangers were reorganized. From Ford's *Memoirs* it is clear he remained on duty. Wallace formed a new company and moved to Fort Inge, as shown by his surviving muster roll. McCulloch formed a new company, according to one of his two remaining muster rolls, and moved to Fredericksburg. These reorganizations and changes suggest the danger area had shifted west away from the Nueces Strip.

This last period of service for these rangers ended in late September 1851. Ford's company was brought to Laredo and discharged in the main plaza on September 23, 1851. The company had served for approximately two years with remarkably few personnel changes, most caused by battle losses. If Ford sounded proud when he bid them good by, he had just cause.

> It may not, perhaps, be considered an infraction of modesty to say, we have done some hard fighting; and have served our Government with zeal, if not with ability. The reputation we have acquired, should be valued beyond price. I trust there is not one of us who will so act as to tarnish our good name, but that each one of us will, on the contrary, use every exertion to sustain it here and elsewhere.[49]

Ford was not alone in his pride in the rangers; most people along the frontier shared his view. They were proud of what had been accomplished and were now worrying about the future after the rangers were discharged. As one editor wrote:

> It is to be hoped that Governor Bell will redeem his promise to give the frontier protection. The ranging companies have done the State good service; the abandoned farms and ranches have been re-settled during their service, and the roads have been freed from the danger to the traveler and merchant. We hope Governor Bell will recall them immediately to protect the frontier, or it will again be devastated and destroyed."[50]

In the coming years, editors would rewrite this plea over and over and over.

THE RANGERS
AS STATE TROOPS

With conditions in Texas as they were—frequent raids from Mexico and the Plains and with the U.S. Army unable to block such attacks—it was inevitable the rangers would be mustered in again. However, for a time the rangers were not the ones on the battle lines; ex-rangers did much of the fighting.

Ford was barely out of service before he was campaigning again, this time in Mexico. In a strict sense, his new campaign has little to do with the history of the rangers, but the combat in late 1851 and early 1852 colored feelings on both sides of the Rio Grande for years to come. The actions of some of the former rangers convinced many that all the rangers were lawless adventurers. Just as many, however, were certain Ford and his followers were patriots trying to free northern Mexico from the chains of a corrupt central government. There were some, including Ford, who also saw the fighting as an opportunity to recapture escaped slaves. He made no apology for this, claiming there were an estimated three-thousand slaves who had escaped to northern Mexico.[1]

The individual who brought about the fighting, called a revolt by some, a disturbance by others, was a Mexican named José María Jesús Carbajal, born in San Antonio and educated in Virginia. He became bitterly opposed to Centralist rule in Mexico and was obsessed with overthrowing the regime.[2] By late 1851, Carbajal had captured Camargo and was appealing to Americans to help him in his "revolt."

In Texas, in addition to wishing to help the Mexicans set up a responsive government and to recover former slaves, there was another interest, purely financial, concerning who controlled the border towns—the men in power were the men who established import duties. For various motives, financial to utopian, many Americans were therefore willing to join with Carbajal. Mustered out on September 23, 1851, Ford crossed into Mexico in October and marched south with some thirty former rangers under the command of Andy Walker. They were well mounted and armed; Ford had personally paid for their accouterments. He was in command of all the auxiliary troops, with the rank of colonel, and a number of other Americans were appointed to senior positions in Carbajal's little army.[3]

It was an ill-fated venture, with little chance for even local success. Carbajal counted on the cooperation of various Mexican commanders, most of whom backed away at critical times. Senior Mexican officers, who understood the role import taxes and smuggling played in border economics and politics, undercut much of Carbajal's popular support.

Now calling themselves a revolutionary army, the combined Texan-Mexican force marched on Matamoros and got into a brisk fight in the town. The Texans played a major role in this fighting, inflicting considerable losses on the town defenders, but Carbajal suddenly withdrew and the Texans had to cover a hasty retreat. The expeditionary force melted away, and the disgruntled Texans returned to their own side of the Rio Grande. There was still considerable sympathy in Texas, but Carbajal had missed his opportunity. By his own admission, Ford had lost much of the respect he had gained from his ranger service; he complained that he was given no credit for his motive.[4]

Part of Carbajal's difficulty arose from his acceptance of American help. Besides the former ranger contingent, he had several Americans as commanders or senior staff officers, and many Mexicans looked on the expedition as another American attack rather than as a revolt against the government in Mexico City. Conditions along the Rio Grande, never good, became worse. The Mexicans were convinced the Texans wanted to take over the region; the Texans were bitter that several prisoners had been executed. With yet another mess to explain, the U.S. government's belief that the Texans were natural born troublemakers was strengthened.

Outsiders often saw the Texans, especially the rangers, as lawless men. In an extreme view, Padre Domenech, a French priest who worked along the Texas frontier and the Rio Grande, considered the rangers the dregs of society, degraded and blood thirsty, mentioning they had massacred Lipans near Castroville, "Rangers, having become the scourge of the colonists, were replaced by regular troops in 1850."[5] Very likely the priest's views were colored by religion, but he did not limit his dislike to the rangers. All Americans—as opposed to "Irish"—were sorry specimens, "The Americans on the frontier were the very scum of society."[6]

The Carbajal affair was a brief moment, along the Rio Grande, whose aftereffects would linger for years. Raids would start again, and there would soon be need for the rangers. Ford, however, would not again be part of the force for some years.

By late summer 1852, Governor Bell was again faced with the necessity of raising forces to protect the frontier, especially the Rio Grande. Naturally, he wished the federal government to pay for the rangers, but the situation was so critical he formed the units and trusted to fate for payment. He directed James S. Gillett, the State Adjutant General, to form three ranger companies.[7]

Bell also wrote President Fillmore and explained the desperate situation in Texas, inclosing appeals from various citizens to bolster his position. The president simply sent the letter and supporting materials to the War Department for action, and the reply from the Secretary of War was not what the governor wanted.[8]

Secretary Conrad began reasonably enough by explaining there were no funds to expand the army, though the need was evident. From then on his letter was patronizing, even arrogantly suggesting the governor was lying! He told Bell that the army officers on the scene found no real Indian danger—in fact the Indians had not been so peaceful in a long time. It might be true some lawless bands roamed the border, mostly Mexican, half breeds and Indians, but there were also considerable numbers of lawless Texans. It was true that some people had been forced to leave their homes because of these people, but it was basically a civil matter. As for the letters submitted, Secretary Conrad informed the governor:

> There is reason to suspect that these statements
> are somewhat exaggerated. Besides the natural ten-

> dency of persons while under the influence of fear to magnify the danger that occasions it, some of the signers of these papers have a strong motive to do so . . . I will merely remark that the Commander of the Department positively pronounces several of the statements contained in them entirely unfounded, and does not recommend that these volunteers be received into the service of the United States.

Continuing to lecture the governor, Conrad pointed out that even if the claims were true, the marauders, Mexican or Texan, were not public enemies the U.S. Army could handle. Such outlaws were the responsibility of the civil powers. If Texas had to raise additional forces to support peace officers, they had the responsibility of paying them.

Additionally, Conrad continued, these disorders had been largely brought about by the citizens of Texas. Referring to the recent Carbajal affair, he said that Texas had to expect Mexican citizens to strike back. Conrad did mention the president felt deeply about the sufferings of "the good people of Texas," and he also mentioned the Department Commander had sent five Mounted Rifle companies to the area, although he admitted there were not enough horses for the troops and no funds to purchase mounts. Conrad did want Bell to know the government had made representations to the Mexican government to stop raiding. He hoped these measures "together with the exercise of a proper degree of vigilance and energy on the part of the citizens and Government of Texas will suffice to restore tranquillity and peace to that region of the country."

Bell was seeking money to pay the rangers rather than permission to call them out. Long before Conrad's insulting letter reached Austin, the units were in service. One company was to be based in Laredo, but Adjutant General Gillett feared it would take a long time to reach the town and there might be a manpower problem. On August 18, 1852, he mustered in a company in San Antonio, commanded by Owen Shaw. The army in San Antonio cooperated by furnishing Gillett everything possible. The Military Department's adjutant general furnished Gillett with copies of organizational outlines for a mounted rifle company, which Gillett used in forming the new ranger unit. The army officer also showed Gillett where army units and posts were located west of San Antonio so that the rangers could work with them.

With one company formed, Gillett rode to Corpus Christi where a second company was to be organized under G.K. Lewis. When he arrived, he discovered Lewis had not received orders and had done nothing. Once officially notified, Lewis went to work, recruiting in Corpus Christi and down in Brownsville. The work went slower than hoped; there were almost no good horses in either town and it was not until September 14 that enough recruits with suitable mounts could be mustered in. Gillett contracted with merchants in Brownsville to supply both this company and the one he expected to form in Rio Grande City.

This third unit, commanded by H. Clay Davis, was mustered in on September 21. Gillett rode up the river to Laredo, where he found Captain Shaw and completed arrangements for supplies both for the organizational period and for future operations. In his detailed report of his actions, Gillett praised the citizens of the districts for their support and cooperation. He said they were in favor of the governor's actions. The men, he believed, were of high caliber, well armed, and he expected good results.[9]

Establishing a camp fifteen miles from Laredo, Shaw was in action before Gillett finished forming the other units. He received information an Indian band had crossed into Texas from Mexico and was sacking ranches as far down river as Roma. The new captain evidently knew the habits of the Indians and made no effort to follow an old trail. He headed for the Nueces, either to intercept the raiders on their return northward or to cut fresh trails.

His instincts were sound. The rangers followed fresh tracks and came upon an Indian camp early in the morning, finding the raiders cooking horse meat. From their sheltered location in a ravine, the Indians saw the approaching Texans and came out to do battle, forming in line and firing at the rangers with rifles, old muskets and one revolver. Shaw deployed his men no more than seventy-five yards away and had his riflemen open fire. The carefully aimed rounds killed the Indian chief in the first volley. Shaw maintained his men under strict control, no man moving or firing unless by command.

Despite superior marksmanship, the rangers were at a disadvantage because the Indians were sheltered by the ravine. Shaw sent one of the guides and a few rangers to separate the Indians from their horses, while a mounted detachment circled behind the Indians. Shaw took fifteen dismounted men and charged the ravine while the other rangers guarded the horses. The rangers had a brisk fight around and in the ravine before they drove the Indians out into the open. The running Indians were intercepted by the mounted Texans, who inflicted some losses. Shaw remounted the rest of his men, and they chased the widely scattered, mostly wounded Indians until a heavy rain flooded the region and fighting or tracking became impossible.

The Indian party had consisted of nineteen men and two women. Nine bodies were left behind, and the rangers believed only one of the warriors was not wounded. They captured twenty-three mules or horses, all saddled, plus blankets and weapons, mostly stolen in Mexico. The rangers had one horse injured.

Since this was the first raid since he had taken over the mission of defending the area, Shaw felt compelled to explain to the governor why he had not intercepted the Indians on their way down. The U.S. Army's Mounted Rifles were in possession of all the water holes below the San Antonio Road, and Shaw naturally assumed they would patrol *between* the holes so he scouted *above* the road, in case the Indians passed through the army pickets. Obviously, they had slipped between the water holes and done the same on the way back to the Plains, where Shaw picked them up.[10]

Shaw's actions indicate a skilled commander, well acquainted with frontier combat. This single fight is all that is really known about his operations, and little more can be learned of the other two companies. Davis has a single surviving report, indicating he also knew how to play the game. He had patrols of fifteen to thirty rangers scouring his area all the time. The work was very arduous but had brought about a complete change in conditions. Before the rangers arrived, raids were commonplace; now they had all but stopped. The day of Davis' report, December 12, 1852, he left for another two weeks' scout.[11]

Muster and pay rolls show Shaw was in service until February 17, 1853. Lewis was mustered out March 13, 1852.[12] While Davis' command was definitely in service, no documents remain to indicate the time or actions taken.

During this period the U.S. Army made some changes in frontier defense in Texas. After General Brooke died in 1851, he was replaced by Major General Persifor F. Smith, who expanded the system of frontier army forts. Smith established a second line, roughly a hundred and fifty miles westward, as well as a number of forts to control the new roads to El Paso del Norte. Since there were no more mounted troops available, this forward displacement accomplished little in the way of halting Indian raids; the Comanches simply continued to ride between the widely separated posts and raid as before. However, one of these forts, Fort Belknap in present day Young County, would become a major base for ranger units.

Governor Bell was succeeded by E.M. Pease, who had some moments of peace during 1853. By 1854, however, conditions were beginning to look like earlier, more turbulent days. Governor Pease suggested local communities defend themselves in an emergency, since they could form minute-man companies or detachments faster than could the state. As soon as possible after the emergency, formal reports would be made to the state's adjutant general of operations and the number of men engaged and their expenses. Pease promised he would "cheerfully recommend that the Legislature make a sufficient appropriation to compensate them for their time and services."[13]

This did not work very well, even for emergencies. Later in 1854 raids again became so extensive that General Smith asked the governor for six ranger companies. These units, officially the Texas Mounted Volunteers, were lettered A through F. The federal government was to furnish ammunition, forage and subsistence. Individual rangers provided their horses, weapons, clothing and equipment. Pay for the men was to be furnished by the United States, providing Congress made the funds available. This would, in effect, make the rangers federal troops, but initially Congress did not make any funds available although the army did provide subsistence.[14] Eventually, after much paperwork, the state ended up paying the men.[15]

Little is known about these six ranger companies. Captain Giles S. Boggess signed a contract with Doctor A. J. Miller promising to pay him one-hundred dollars a month to be surgeon of Company A.[16] Muster rolls for all units, except Company E, commanded by

Captain C. E. Travis, are in the Ranger Papers in the Texas State Library, another indication these were not federal troops despite the method in which they were called to duty.[17]

A little more is known about Captain William R. Henry's company. Formed in Goliad, it was assigned to Fort Clark, one of the new posts established by direction of General Smith. In a letter to Governor Pease, Henry explained he had to send two men on express to Clark to gather his company for muster into the service of the United States.[18] The unit must have done some scouting, because there is a voucher for shoeing horses for his command.[19]

Not all of Henry's actions seemed to be directed towards frontier defense, and there are serious questions about the discipline in his command. A newspaper story described how some rangers stationed near D'Hanis shot up sign boards and the local post office, scattering mail and killing two hogs. The detachment was supposedly under the command of a Lieutenant Jackson, who was nice enough and well liked by the townspeople but who unfortunately had no control over his men. The local citizens wanted rangers, but not these mounted volunteers. The Indians' theft of valuable horses and cattle, and even killing people, could be endured better than the actions of the men who were supposed to protect them.[20]

The rangers are not identified, but an examination of Henry's muster roll shows a Lieutenant Jackson who was relieved and confined.[21] There was some complaint about Henry's scouting into Mexico, which was outside his mission. Still, his company was one of the three companies retained on active service by General Smith when the other three disbanded.[22] It was a temporary reprieve; the three remaining units were also mustered out by the end of March or early April 1855.

—4—
CALLAHAN'S RAID

There was a sharp increase in Indian attacks along the southwestern Texas frontier during the early summer of 1855, and petitions and calls for help were almost an everyday occurrence in the governor's office. Recounting these in detail would be tedious, but there was agreement that something had to be done to help the exposed settlers or see the frontier collapse.[1] One particularly expressive petition was sent from San Antonio in early July and summarized Indian activity from late 1854 to the present. An especially alarming feature of the petition was the large number of people who had been killed just in the area around San Antonio. A lengthy list of people signed the call for help, a cry raised not by merely a few frightened farmers but by a broad section of the community, including Hispanics. They asked for a ranger company and recommended either G.W. Tobin or Marcellus French as commander.[2]

Impassioned as this plea was, it was not the factor that led Governor Pease to form a new company although it probably did influence him as to the location of the unit. An especially gruesome Indian murder, a month earlier, was the event that really brought about a new ranger company.

In June 1855 a raiding party swept through west Guadalupe County and down the Cibolo valley. They stole horses from near the residence of James McKee and killed a negro caught in the open. When they came across young Doc McKee and Pendleton Rector, who were out riding and tried to escape, Rector's horse fell, throwing him, but he managed to hide in a thicket. The Indians caught his horse and started after McKee. The young man was riding a mule and soon overtaken, "roped, dragged to the ground, lanced and scalped."[3]

The young man was well known and popular, the son of a

Methodist minister. His death, as well as that of the slave, and the heavy stock losses inflamed the region. Henry McCulloch raised a volunteer posse and chased the raiders, without success. Newspapers carried stories on the murder and the raid. Governor Pease, under considerable pressure to do something to prevent future attacks, wrote General Smith, calling his attention to stories in the *State Times* and pointing out the murder took place in an area where there were no mounted troops. Knowing there was no defense or organized pursuit to face, the Indians had become bolder. The governor was afraid future attacks would encourage the citizens to arm and attack any Indians they could find, leading to a general Indian war. Pease said the solution was to station a company of mounted soldiers in the vicinity.[4]

Whatever he might have wished, Smith had no mounted soldiers to spare. Pease then called on James Callahan to form a ranger company, informing him the people on the Guadalupe and tributaries in Bexar and Comal counties required protection. Since the U.S. Army could not help, he was authorizing Callahan to form a company for three months.[5]

The governor authorized a unit not to exceed the size of a mounted company in the United States service. He was honest with Callahan, telling him there was no money to pay for anything, not even forage, horses, arms or ammunition, much less to pay the rangers. Anyone's enlisting must know this and be able to support himself until the legislature could reimburse him the usual amount paid to U.S. military servicemen.

If Callahan could form a company under these circumstances, he was to furnish the governor's office with muster rolls then move to near the endangered settlements for their protection. Pease continued with instructions that would lead to some startling events.

> It is expected that you will be actively engaged in rangeing in their vicinity, unless it may become necessary to pursue any marauding parties of Indians that may be found in the neighborhood, in which case you are authorized to follow up and chastise them wherever they may be found.

Pease specifically cautioned Callahan about attacking peaceful Indians, trespassing upon property, or injuring citizens. Lastly, he mentioned that if General Smith could furnish troops, Callahan's company would be disbanded.

Just why Pease selected Callahan is not known, but it seemed a good choice. Callahan had fought in the Texas Revolution and had been one of the few to escape the Goliad massacre. Later he commanded volunteer ranging companies and saw considerable service during the days of

Governor E.M. Pease

the Texas Republic.[6] He lived in the threatened area and knew the country.

From his letter, Pease had doubts about Callahan's being able to form a company under a fight-without-pay handicap. However, volunteers arrived from all over the threatened area and, on July 20, Callahan swore in the authorized two lieutenants, four sergeants, four corporals, two buglers, a farrier, and eighty-five rather than seventy-four privates. At forty, Callahan was the second oldest man in the company. First Bugler John McCoy was sixteen, the youngest. First Corporal Charles Taylor was eighteen, as were six others. There were a few older men in their thirties or more, but most of the new rangers were in their teens or early twenties.[7]

Unaware of how easily Callahan had formed a company of even more than the authorized strength, the governor wrote him on July 25, undoubtedly as a result of the petition from the citizens of Bexar County. He doubted another company could be formed and suggested Callahan split his company and furnish protection to the additional area. He said General Smith had promised a Mounted Rifle company, but he doubted help would come soon. Pease suggested recruits might be obtained in San Antonio and Castroville if it was known the new company would defend these towns. The knowledge would also help in obtaining supplies in each place.[8] The same day, Pease sent a letter to the citizens of Bexar County informing them of the authorization for Callahan's company and his order to station some of the new rangers to protect Bexar and Medina counties. He promised if these men were not enough, he would not hesitate to call out additional volunteers.[9] The governor was well aware of the political implications of angry and frightened citizens' believing their governor was abandoning them. Providing defense for the frontier would be a growing burden for Texas governors and would lead directly to one of them being voted out of office.

Captain Callahan probably had little thought for the politics of frontier defense. Forming his new company had been easy enough; feeding and supplying the men was another matter. On August 1 he issued Order No. 1 instructing Lieutenant Ed Burleson to go either to Austin or San Antonio and contract for supplies. Burleson went first to Austin, where Governor Pease added an endorsement of sorts to the order, telling whomever might read it that he had authorized the mustering in of the company and that, although there was at yet no appropriation, finances would be taken care of.[10]

Burleson must have found supplies in San Antonio, because he returned to the company and the rangers remained on duty. The company soon moved to Bandera and established a camp; the exact date is unknown, but on September 15 Burleson made another trip, this time to Austin.[11] Callahan rented two small buildings in Bandera, one for a commissary and the other for a hospital, so apparently there was no major problem in obtaining new supplies. Rent was paid for seven weeks, although again the exact dates are unknown.[12] The rangers were active, because in the archives are several vouchers for expenses claimed by blacksmiths for shoeing horses.[13]

Other reports also show Callahan's men were busy. In a long letter to Governor Pease, W.E. Jones reported on conditions along the frontier and gave some details about the new ranger company. A patrol had trailed a small Indian band in late August and wounded two and captured all their horses and gear. On September 7 another patrol overtook a small raiding band, killing one and wounding two others, again capturing many horses. Jones had visited Callahan in mid-September, finding half of the rangers northeast of

Fredericksburg and the remainder along the Guadalupe River. Callahan believed none of the raiders had penetrated his patrol line and thought the attacks had come from the south. In each encounter, the fleeing Indians had run towards San Antonio and Mexico. Jones concluded by mentioning Callahan was preparing for a major scout with most of his company.[14] The ranger captain was not alone in suspecting Indian attacks were originating in Mexico; newspaper stories indicated the raiders were concentrated in Mexico, opposite Eagle Pass.[15]

While Callahan's rangers were evidently doing a good job, there was always pressure for more protection. In addition, some would-be ranger captains were looking for work; on September 2, 1855, W.R. Henry sent a long letter to the governor asking for the command of a new company.[16] Henry reminded Pease of the petition from the citizens of the area "for the purpose of presenting my claims for the organization and command of said company."

He went on to fill three pages explaining that he was aware of the delicate situation Pease was in, having to decide among many candidates. All he asked was a fair chance to form a company and let the men elect their captain. He also hoped the governor knew how much he admired him and what a loyal supporter he had been. Henry made a special point of asking the governor not to make a judgment based on his last campaign—there had been no opportunity to do anything. He modestly admitted he had a knowledge of military matters. If there was no company command to be had, he would accept anything because he had a family to support. He concluded by again flattering the governor and by justifying his previous Mexican involvement by saying he knew in his heart he had helped a downtrodden people cast off the yoke of tyranny.

Pease was in a critical situation and did not need a self-serving letter from a questionable commander at this time. The pressures on him must have been considerable, and he turned to the most obvious source of aid; the governor went to San Antonio to confer with General Smith. When he reached town, Pease found the general was in Corpus Christi and not expected back before the end of the month. Since Pease could not wait in San Antonio for several weeks, he wrote General Smith a long letter describing conditions and the need for help.[17]

Once again, the murder of Doc McKee was used as a starting point. Pease expounded on the killings and the thefts of cattle and horses, reminding Smith that others had written repeatedly about conditions along the frontier. He reported that the company called out earlier under Callahan had done fine work and halted Indian raids in their area. Pease reminded the general that, as governor, he was in a difficult situation; if he were forced to call out volunteers, they could overreact and punish all Indians, undermining the efforts being made to settle the Texas tribes on reservations. He pleaded with the Department Commander to furnish a company or two of mounted men to defend the Frio/Llano region before the settlements broke up. He promised to defer action until he heard from the general.

Pease was attempting to appease desperate and frightened citizens while doing what little he could to provide protection. He evidently brought correspondence with him to San Antonio because, the day after he wrote to General Smith, he answered a letter he must have considered critical. Noting he had their letter with its further accounts of Indian raids and the proceedings of a public meeting, Pease explained to the three signers that he expected to hear from General Smith in a few days. If he did not, he promised to call out a volunteer company until the legislature could assemble and take some action.[18]

There was, however, to be no increase in U.S. Army support; all that changed was an increase in Indian attacks. Indians raided along the Blanco River, stealing horses and killing livestock. Comal County settlers held a meeting in New Braunfels on September 12 to consider defensive measures. Despite their location almost a hundred miles behind the so-called frontier, they were being raided.[19]

If General Smith made any direct reply to Pease it has not survived, but he did remain in touch with his higher headquarters. He reported to the army's adjutant general during this time that Indians, supposedly Lipan, had been crossing the border and stealing horses. He explained that late rains made trailing impossible, though the Mounted Rifles had tried to intercept the invaders.[20]

During this confused time in early September, Callahan seemed the only one who had any plan. He began by preparing for a major strike. On September 12, 1855, he issued Special Orders No. 2, again to Lieutenant Burleson now listed as 1st Lt & Q Master, telling him that, "Sir you will proceed to San Antonio immediately and make any arrangements you can in order to get me as many as fifteen hundred and sixty Rations each of Flour and Bacon."[21]

Burleson went to San Antonio for the supplies, from where he wrote Governor Pease on September 15 informing him that the company was on a scout, after Lipans in particular, "wherever we may find them." Somewhere in this time frame, J.S. McDowell, a member of the company, began making notes on daily events.[22]

Callahan had already moved out, halting on the Leona River where additional fresh trails were found suggesting a large force. Callahan decided he needed help so as not to leave the region undefended and sent calls for assistance to San Antonio and Seguin, the nearest towns. Nat Benton rode over from Seguin with thirty men. Henry, seeing his chance, gathered about the same number in San Antonio and joined Callahan.[23]

The combined units decided to hold an election to select a battalion commander. Callahan was the winner, but there was a dispute between Benton and Henry over who would command the second company. Henry won in a close contest but the election was challenged; not all the men approved of his earlier raid into Mexico. Another election was held for the commander of the third company, and on September 26 Nat Benton was elected commander of the new, thirty-five man company, about the same size as the one under Henry. Callahan, retaining command of one of the three companies as well as over-all command, had about sixty men after he detached twenty-six rangers to defend their old area.[24]

Callahan addressed the newly organized command. He told them he was acting under the orders of the governor, considered it a privilege, and was going to obey his orders to the letter. If they crossed the Rio Grande, they would do so only to chase and punish Indians. They were not to harm any Mexican citizens or take their property; if any man expected to act otherwise, he should leave or face punishment. The speech seemed to meet with general approval.

The command moved to the Nueces, where scouts found them and told of fresh tracks, leading to the Rio Grande, which the Texans followed to the river. The scouts said the Indian camp, with many stolen horses, was about nine miles away. On the river by September 29, Callahan was unable to cross because of high, swift water. He

Eagle Pass, Texas, about 1855, from a contemporary engraving. This shows the
countryside near Fort Duncan. Clearly depicted are the considerable bluffs
along the Rio Grande, a terrain feature of importance during Callahan's Raid.

experimented with makeshift rafts, but they were too dangerous and
abandoned. At this point, new intelligence arrived concerning a Lipan
camp inland from Piedras Negras, near San Fernando. Callahan
decided to move down river to Eagle Pass, cross the river and attack
this camp because, from the evidence he had, it seemed likely the
raids into Texas had originated there.

Starting down river about dusk on the last day of September, the
Texans marched all night and arrived about four miles north of Eagle
Pass the following evening. Establishing a camp, Callahan took Henry
and Benton and rode into town. McDowell did not know with whom
they dealt, but he remembered they returned with assurances there
would be boats to carry the rangers across into Mexico. Henry and
ten men were sent back yet again to bring the boats from the Mexican
side.

Despite his authorization from the governor, Callahan was worried about the reaction of the army garrison at nearby Fort Duncan.
The Texans circled Eagle Pass and reached the riverbank three miles
below the army post. Matters appeared to be going according to plan
when two skiffs arrived on the Texas shore. Henry and a few men

View of Fort Duncan, near Eagle Pass, from a contemporary engraving.

started across. Close to the Mexican side, Henry yelled that some Mexicans had followed him and were threatening to attack. Hearing this, about thirty of the rangers managed to row across the rough current, disembarked and formed a skirmish line on the opposite bank. When several hours passed without incident, half of the men returned to the Texas side, leaving the others to guard the landing site.

Early in the morning of October 1, a delegation from Piedras Negras visited the Texans on the Mexican side and asked their intentions. The rangers assured them they were interested solely in punishing the Indians who had raided into Texas and had no designs on Mexican lives or property. The assurances seemed to satisfy the Mexican citizens and, according to McDowell, they offered their help in crossing the Rio Grande and fighting the Indians. He said the rangers accepted the offer of help only for crossing the Rio Grande.

The rangers spent all day crossing into Mexico. They had to swim across their horses in small groups while the men were rowed over a few at a time. There was no interference with the "invasion." Callahan later told Pease that Emilio Langberg, the military commander of the state of Coahuila, had written him a note interposing no objection to the attack on the Indians.[25] On the morning of October 3, Callahan had 115 men on the Mexican side of the Rio

Grande. Six rangers were too sick to ride, and it was necessary to leave a guard with the extra horses and equipment and supplies.

Callahan led his men down the road to San Fernando the morning of October 3, resting at noon on a stream bank about fifteen miles south of Piedras Negras. After eating they started again, moving at a brisk walk, and after another eight or nine miles they met a Mexican rider who warned them they were expected. The Texans distrusted anyone south of the river and remained on the road.

If the rangers had any scouts out, they must have been dozing in the saddle; the country, open on all sides, may have given the Texans a false sense of security. A few men noticed dust in and around a stand of timber about 250 yards to the right of the road, but there were cattle in the vicinity and the rangers assumed the dust had been raised by the cows. However, when they were opposite the timber, they saw men and horses and sunlight reflected from weapons, and the easygoing joking and talking stopped abruptly. Three Indians rode from the woods, all finely dressed; McDowell thought at least two were chiefs. The rangers formed into a line facing the woods and dismounted, after which an Indian force estimated at 150 to 200 warriors filed from the trees and formed a long line facing the Texans. One of the chiefs rode about trying to draw the rangers out of position or bring on a premature burst of firing, but the rangers were instructed to stand fast and merely watched the chief gallop about before them. Becoming bolder, he rode even closer and shot an arrow over the Texans. Two rangers fired and hit the Indian's horse, but the chief managed to regain the shelter of the woods.

While this was taking place, the three captains had been discussing plans. As they watched, a file of footmen, mostly Mexicans, left the trees and formed at right angles to the Indians and the rangers. McDowell believed this group numbered from two to three hundred, which was probably high. Whatever the actual figure, the Texans were considerably outnumbered.

Callahan fell back on an old tactic from the Republic days when revolvers were not yet in use. The rangers would charge, fire, and then retreat to a ravine and use the banks as a shelter. Some men would reload while others fired to maintain a steady barrage. Since there were a number of revolvers scattered among the companies, Callahan elected to ride straight at one arm of the L-shaped formation rather than attack from the side.

The rangers did as commanded and charged straight ahead at the Indians, exposing themselves to a possible flanking fire from the Mexican line. They held their fire until almost upon the Indians and blasted a way through the formation. The Indians gave way at the first rush and, for some reason, the Mexicans became confused and failed to strike the exposed ranger flank. The Mexicans also started to fall back, but Callahan and the other commanders lost control and failed to seize the opportunity. Instead, they led their men, as planned, back to a stream bed and dismounted.

It had been a brief and bloody melee for a moment. The rangers had four men killed and seven wounded in shattering the two enemy lines, as well as some loss of mounts, but they estimated they had killed some thirty men, mostly Indian. While these figures are impressive, they lost the chance to scatter the two bands completely and inflict heavy casualties in a pursuit. While Callahan was supervising the securing of horses and the establishing of a defensive position in the ravine, the enemy had plenty of time to rally and resume the fight.

The Indians set fire to the tall grass, trying to burn the Texans out of their shelter, but when this failed several Indians crept through what was left of the grass and opened fire. This was an old game to the rangers who responded in kind, killing and wounding most of the attackers.

One of the Texans, Fabian L. Hicks, recalled the day many years later.[26] During the charge, he fired his double-barreled shot gun at a Mexican soldier, who "squatted" down at the moment of firing so that the buckshot flew over his head. The disgruntled Hicks turned and discharged the second round directly into an Indian, who collapsed. Like the other uninjured, Hicks reached the shelter of the ravine and continued the fight.

Captain Nat Benton was wounded but managed to reach the ravine. He was worried about his son, who had been shot and unhorsed and was out in the burning grass. Hicks, Wesley Harris and Hughes Tom decided to save their friend, and the three young rangers crawled out under considerable fire and managed to drag young Benton to safety. It was a gallant act which partially made up for the Mexican recovery of the four dead rangers.

Isolated firing continued until near sunset when the Mexicans and Indians began drifting away towards San Fernando. The battle of Escondido was over.

Both sides claimed victory as soon as they reached shelter. The Mexican commander admitted losing four killed and three wounded, absurdly low figures. Texas estimates on the field were about thirty enemy dead, largely Indian. Later, based on Mexican accounts, the figure rose to fifty-six then to ninety. The Texans lost four dead and seven wounded, a not insignificant total.

McDowell had the figures of four dead and seven wounded but was not certain of names other than that of a man named Jones and the names of about half of the wounded. Muster rolls for all three ranger units survive, and a comparison of rolls and casualties identifies the dead rangers as Willis H. Jones, a member of Henry's company, H.K. Holland from Benton's unit, and William H. Clopton and Augustus Smith of Callahan's company.

These four men, listed on muster rolls, agree with accounts of four deaths at Escondido. There is a fifth name, Samuel G. Smith of Callahan's company, with the notation "killed," but it seems likely this was either a clerical error or he died elsewhere than in this fight in Mexico. Young Benton was initially listed as killed but the notation was changed to wounded. All the dead from the fight are listed as "killed at Escondido," or "killed 3 October."

Identifying the wounded is more difficult. Eustice Benton, Benjamin Patton and Polk R. Kyle, all from Callahan's company, are listed as wounded at Escondido. From eyewitness accounts, Nat Benton was wounded although he is not listed as such on his company's muster roll. Lieutenant Henry King was also a known injured but is not listed. McDowell remembered a Wright and a Bonner's being hurt, even the specific wounds; R.M. Bonner was in Benton's company and E.M. Wright was in Callahan's unit. Possibly, whoever kept the records mentioned only deaths and serious injuries.

The casualties were spread throughout the three companies. Callahan suffered the heaviest loss, but he commanded almost half the men in the fight.

Around noon on October 4, the commander of the garrison at Fort Duncan wrote an urgent dispatch to Department Headquarters in San Antonio stating that armed Texans had invaded Mexico three night earlier, evidently planning to chastise Lipans for raiding in

Texas. The crossing had been made without his knowledge or consent. The encamped Texans had departed their base the previous day and marched towards San Fernando. There had been a fight, with some known dead and injured among the Texans. Stories were conflicting—a wounded straggler had recrossed the river and said a large Mexican force had attacked and probably killed all the Texans. That morning he had received repeated calls from survivors of the fight for help in crossing the Rio Grande.

Captain S. Burbank, 1st Infantry, commanding little more than a detachment of United States troops, was in a delicate situation. He explained in this report that he considered it his duty to aid the Texas withdrawal and had placed artillery to cover the river crossing. After several hours passed with no sign of Indian or Mexican attack, he had learned the Texans had captured Piedras Negras! He believed they proposed holding the town until reinforcements arrived. Burbank concluded:

> As this matter is likely to become quite serious, the Texans on hearing of the situation of their countrymen and of the death of their friends will flock to the frontier in large numbers and will cross the river in spite of resistance. I respectfully beg leave to ask instructions for the government of my action in this matter. If the Texans should persist in crossing, acting under orders of the Governor as they appear to be doing, I have no force sufficient to oppose them, admitting it my duty to do so. If some persons of standing and influence do not immediately interfere, open war must follow in a very short time.[27]

Completely unaware of the potentially disastrous situation on the Rio Grande, Governor Pease wrote a short message to Ed Burleson who was commanding the detachment left behind by Callahan. Pease said that General Smith had finally promised some troopers from the Mounted Rifles to defend the frontier, and therefore Callahan's rangers would be mustered out when their three months service was finished. They were instructed to ride to San Marcos for discharge.[28] The same day, October 4, Callahan found time to report what had happened, but his report has not survived.[29]

A great deal had happened, but the real trouble was ahead. It must have taken the rangers a considerable time to regroup following the retreat of the enemy. They had lost some horses and there were wounded to transport. They rode during the night and camped near Piedras Negras about three the morning after the fight on October 4. Why they did not begin to recross the Rio Grande is a matter of dispute. McDowell never explained or tried to justify remaining near the Mexican town, just as he failed to comment on Callahan's demand for the surrender of Piedras Negras. There was no argument from within the town; a delegation came out and gave up without protest even though there were two-thousand people in town and only slightly more than one-hundred battle-weary rangers.

During daylight, the Texans rode into town and made their headquarters in a small stone fort. The alcalde arrived to surrender the keys of the town, promising to turn in all arms in the place. In short order, the Texans had a pile of weapons of every description, age and condition, including two cannon. They took the opportunity to eat and get some sleep but were careful not to take anything other than food. Guards were posted, and rangers and citizens spent a quiet night.

During the day, Callahan sent his wounded across to Eagle Pass for medical treatment. McDowell accompanied them, staying on the Texas side, and again there is no explanation why Callahan remained another twenty-four hours in Mexico. Years later McDowell believed it could have been because Callahan was angry that the Mexicans had promised to support him and instead had fought side-by-side with the Indians. The rangers had heard that ninety Indian and Mexican fighters had been killed the day before, with many wounded. Callahan may also have believed reinforcements would ride to join him if he stayed. Whatever his reason, the Texan held fast and ordered the erection of barricades in the streets of Piedras Negras.

When rumors began flying through the town that fourteen-hundred men were on the way to attack the Texans, who now numbered about ninety in Piedras Negras after escorts for the wounded, guards for the horses on the opposite shore and other details had reduced the command, Callahan asked Burbank for help in crossing the river. The disgruntled officer told the ranger they had refused his original offer and could get back on their own.

It was later claimed the rangers set fire to shacks and fences on the outskirts of Piedras Negras to slow the advance of the army they believed was approaching. Under cover of the smoke, they moved to the bluff along the Rio Grande, still in flood stage with waters too deep and too swift to ford. The only safe way across was by boat, and the rangers started across using whatever they could find that would float. A yawl, with fifteen men aboard, broke loose but finally landed on the American shore. A number of the men attempted to swim with their horses, but not all were able to save their mounts and thirty horses remained tied under the shelter of the bluff on a narrow sand bar. McDowell and two companions rowed back over in an unsuccessful attempt to save their mounts, but most of these animals were left behind. There was no attempt to attack or harry the retreating rangers, who were all across by the morning of October 7, 1855.

The rangers assembled in Eagle Pass, less many of their horses but with considerable stores of corn, flour and produce from across the Rio Grande. One citizen of Eagle Pass claimed he saw some men wearing gold jewelry.[30] Unfortunately, most of Piedras Negras burned to the ground, and early in the day Mexican troops occupied the town ruins.

Captain Burbank's version of events in his follow-up report to his superiors on October 8 agrees closely with McDowell's recollection, but with additional details. He thought the Texans stayed in Mexico on October 4 because the river was too high to bring their horses across; when the river fell somewhat on October 6 the Texans sent over some of their horses. Burbank reported he had received a note, supposedly from the Mexican commander asking what his position was regarding the rangers, but he did not reply.

Burbank said he thought the rangers were all crossing, but around four in the afternoon some Mexican troops were seen advancing on the town and the remaining rangers set fire to Piedras Negras. Burbank verified that Callahan had sent a message requesting help, but that he had refused both this and a second request. He explained he believed the Texans had enough boats to cross the men and could lose their horses. He described the wild ride of the barge, as mentioned by McDowell, and thought most of the Texans were on the American side by two o'clock the morning of October 8. They had camped somewhere in the vicinity.

The officer reported to Department Headquarters that the citizens of Piedras Negras were in desperate condition and suggested provisions should be made to help the most needy. The Mexicans were threatening revenge. People in Eagle Pass were frightened, and he had to post guards in the town during the night. Burbank confirmed that there were many Seminoles with the Mexicans. He concluded that conditions would probably calm down unless the Texans sent reinforcements. Again, he asked guidance on how to deal with another invasion.[31]

The fighting was over. McDowell borrowed a horse from the expedition surgeon and started for San Antonio with two friends. Others began drifting north. The rangers had played their part, and now the diplomats and the politicians moved to center stage.

Knowing only what Callahan wrote him the day after the fight at Escondido, the governor answered the ranger quickly, telling Callahan he was justified in following the Indians into Mexico in the hope of recovering stolen property and to punish them, but

> you had not the right to take possession or occupy
> Piedras Negras or any other village or property of
> Mexican Citizens; after the termination of your
> engagement with the Indians, you should have
> returned immediately to this side of the Rio Grande,
> and I trust that you have already done so.

Pease commended Callahan for defeating a superior force and commanded him to return if he had not already done so. He finished by hoping the ranger had committed no acts that would give the citizens of Mexico cause for complaint.[32] It must have been a considerable shock to Pease when he learned the complete story of the raid!

Whatever his feelings, Pease was loyal and, a few days later, wrote General Smith to defend the rangers. He stressed he had no objection to Callahan's entering Mexico, only to the occupation of Piedras Negras. The governor told the general no one would regret a border war more than he would, but the fault would be with the federal government for not furnishing adequate protection.[33]

Pease's letter was too much for a mere Department Commander, and Smith bucked the matter to Washington. Smith said he was worried about the number of Texans who were riding into San Antonio to form an expedition to invade Mexico, noting they were "well armed and mounted and of a much better class of citizens than usually join in such expeditions."[34]

Sarcastically, he wondered how areas that were crying for protection could send three times the strength of the U.S. Army in the entire state on such a venture. Smith promised he would do what he could to prevent any invasion, but he admitted that Indians were constantly raiding and that any band of Texans could justly claim they were chasing marauders into Mexico. He pointed out such Indian raids along the Rio Grande drew troops that were also needed along the inland frontier. He promised to do what he could to control matters, and he believed matters would cool down because the more prudent citizens were abandoning the expedition.[35]

Pease wasted no time in discharging the rangers in the three companies. He directed Colonel John D. Pitts to muster out Callahan's company when it was presented to him and to furnish original muster rolls. There was no money for pay, but he wanted Callahan to furnish a statement of expenses and supplies furnished.[36] Muster and pay rolls show Callahan's company left service October 19, 1855; the other two units were discharged even earlier on October 15.[37]

During this period, one of the officers in the new 2nd Cavalry Regiment wrote the governor that the unit might not reach Texas in the fall as scheduled. Pease immediately wrote General Smith and asked for help, stating than an attack by Lipan and Seminoles was likely, and the danger could be averted by Smith's requesting Texas to form volunteer troops. Not surprisingly, Smith made no such request.[38]

Pease had formed Callahan's company in good faith, promising to pay the rangers when there was money available. He also felt an obligation to reimburse the men who followed Benton and Henry, even if their companies had not been officially sanctioned. He raised the question of pay when the legislature met, outlining the propriety of payment for service, supplies expended, lost animals and weapons, etc.[39]

The legislature passed an act to reimburse the rangers on December 17, 1855, and Pease ordered the men paid in San

Marcos.[40] McDowell's notes show he was paid $149 for service and a lost horse, but he does not indicate just when he was paid. Determining pay for time in service was easy enough, but trying to find how many and the value of the animals lost was difficult. The three company commanders finally had to turn in affidavits for every ranger who made any claim, and the notations on muster rolls do not always match later individual claims. There was a general agreement that property losses had been heavy. Callahan's muster roll shows twenty-four horses and pack mules missing. Eleven men lost weapons. Benton showed a number of missing horses, including two belonging to casualties in his unit. Henry lost his personal mount, as well as thirteen others in his company, plus a considerable number of weapons. Individual claims were still being submitted in 1857![41]

Efforts to settle ranger claims lasted for several years, but not as long as those of the Mexicans with damages claimed from the fire in Piedras Negras. The often divided Mexicans united on the issue of their claims and demands to Washington, and they made a point that their sovereignty had been violated. They asked for everything from punishment of Captain Buchanan for not stopping the invasion to monetary compensation for a multitude of losses.[42]

The only facet of Callahan's raid that continued longer than trying to settle claims was the still lingering question of why he crossed into Mexico. The official justification was that he was in pursuit of Lipan raiders as authorized by Governor Pease. However, at the time there was some belief he was also interested in the return of ex-slaves. This view must have been sufficiently prevalent for a traveler to hear of it often enough to conclude it was the *main* reason, as Frederick Olmstead did in his account of his stay in Texas.[43]

There was great concern about runaway slaves in 1850 Texas. Although there were few slaves in the frontier counties, the economy of East Texas was dependent on slave labor, and the plantation system, largely based on cotton, had a significant impact on the state's economy. If a slave managed to escape into the frontier area, he stood a good chance of making the rest of the trip into Mexico where he was free, and many risked the danger and hardship of the long trip. The losses to the eastern plantation owners were considerable, and they made it financially worthwhile for people in the frontier regions to catch and return slaves. During the summer of 1855, meetings were held in Bastrop, newspapers in the area active in the effort to stop fleeing slaves,[44] and some of the influential citizens were interested in breaking up the exodus from Texas. John Ford developed a plan, working with Colonel B. Riddle, and the two men were appointed agents to work with revolutionary Mexican officials in a scheme to halt the escape of slaves into Mexico and return slaves from that country.[45]

The only definite thing about this "plan" was the division of responsibility: Ford was to work with officials in Matamoros while Riddle would have the territory further west in Chihuahua.[46] Callahan did mention Riddle in a letter to Governor Pease, saying he had met him and discussed cooperation with various Mexican authorities—and possibly even revolutionists—who would be encouraged to collect ex-slaves for return to Texas.[47] The hazy plan collapsed when Callahan's rangers crossed the Rio Grande and everyone, governmental and revolutionaries, rallied against the *gringos*. There was so much hostility against anything American that Ford was afraid to visit Matamoros for discussions.

The case for Callahan's invasion being motivated by the desire to recapture ex-slaves rests on such evidence and is neither strong nor convincing. At no time in any of his talks to the rangers did he mention the return of slaves as part of their mission. Nor did any of the men who made notes at the time, or who later wrote their recollections, mention this as a justification for the raid. Callahan did talk with Riddle about the possibility, but going into Mexico after former slaves would have been futile unless Mexican authorities had already and forcibly rounded up a sizable number and made arrangements to deliver them to the rangers. Despite their internal conflicts, all the Mexican factions abided by the prohibition against slavery in their constitutions. Callahan discovered this when he believed he had been promised support but found he faced both Indians and Mexican troops on October 3.

Whatever his motive, people in Texas in 1855 generally believed Callahan was justified in crossing the Rio Grande. He was defended in the papers and praised in public. Making no further effort to serve as a ranger or with any other public organization, Callahan left his old home in Seguin and moved to the present day town of Blanco. On April 7, 1856, Callahan and two friends rode to a neighbor's farm where he was killed during an argument that apparently had nothing to do with his ranger service. His death outraged old friends in Seguin who, handling the matter without bothering civil authorities, rode over to Blanco and shot the people who had murdered him. Grateful citizens saw that the legislature named a new county for Callahan in the session of 1856-1857. He and his wife were reburied in the State Cemetery in 1931.

The furor over his raid had begun to die down even before Callahan was killed, although some hotheads and a few editors attempted to keep the pot boiling for a time. Some of the papers blamed the burning of Piedras Negras on the Mexicans, a just reward for their treachery when they changed sides. One paper claimed the ranger dead were carried to San Fernando for dissection, a wild claim that briefly infuriated some people. There was even a call for yet another invasion of Mexico by a large expedition to assemble on November 15 on the Cibolo near the mouth of the Santa Clara.[48] Another invasion made sense to some people for a time, and The *San Antonio Sentinel* even justified the invasion by the artful statement that there had never been any real violation of neutrality laws because Mexico did not have a real government.[49]

No expedition formed on the Cibolo, and the people along the frontier returned to the day-to-day business of trying to stay alive.

—5—
NEW YEAR -
OLD PROBLEMS

C allahan's raid, the main incident for the rangers in 1855, was one of several of the "big events" of the decade, a time when conditions along the Texas frontier were seldom under control. Considering the number of ranger units involved and the turmoil created, something more lasting in results might have been expected. It is no reflection on the men engaged to note conditions did not improve, and that the rangers would be trying to solve the same problems for decades to come.

Governor Pease continued to call up ranger units to meet scattered threats. The exceptional big raid and battle gave way to the more normal small patrol and scouting activities that characterized the period. In the final months of 1855, William Tom and William G. Tobin commanded ranger companies for short periods. Levi English led a unit from August 6 to November 13, 1855, and had several skirmishes with Lipans.[1] When the new year arrived, Pease called for additional companies to meet local emergencies; J.W. Sansom, John M. Davenport and Reading Black served as company commanders in these new units.[2]

Indian attacks were not as intense during 1856 as in earlier years, but there was a continuing need for ranger forces. There are eight surviving muster rolls in the State Archives for 1856-1857, but otherwise there is little documentation for what was actually accomplished.

John Davenport led a thirty-seven man company from March 13, 1856, until June 1, 1857, one of the few units that left any record of service other than muster and pay rolls. Captain Davenport used one of the printed forms available at the time showing names and dates of service, with space for remarks on the back. Under "kinds of service," the ranger wrote "Scouting and Fighting." In the notation of a fight in the Frio Mountains, opposite one name is a notation the ranger was wounded by six arrows on June 8, 1856, and another ranger was hit by rifle fire the same day.[3] Davenport maintained a record of major scouts during 1856 on the back of his muster roll.

General Remarks
1st

On the 20th day of March 1856, a party of Indians, supposed to be Comanches, came into the lower Sabinal Settlements and stole 7 head of horses and mules. I took the trail with my men which was followed up to the head waters of the new Esses, then crossing we proceeded to the south prong of the Llano, and on arriving there late in the afternoon, discovered the Indians encamped barbacuing a horse. We charged the Camp, but being on an elevated position and the Indians in a low ravine, discovered our movement and made their escape through a Mountain pass, being then dark, and in the morning no trail was available –

Scout 2nd

On the night of the 16th day of May, a party of Comanchy Indians 8 in number came into old Fort Lincoln and stole 8 head of horses. We took their trail next morning and followed them to the head waters of the Medina river, but owing to a heavy rain, we lossed the trail and could not proceed any further.

Scout 3rd

On the night of 7th June 1856 there was a party of Indians supposed to be 25 in number came into the upper Sabinal settlements, known as Canion Valley, five of them entering the yard of Mr Aron Anglon and killed two dogs, being fired on by John Leaky a private of my Company, who was stopping for the night in Mr Anglons house and from his exertions the Indians left the yard. I sent five men next morning to hunt for their trail while I was collecting the balance of the men about three miles south west from Anglons house. the above mentioned five men came on the Indians in Camp on the Frio Mountains this being the place where Mr. Leaky and Baremore received their wounds. On the morning of the 9th I took the trail with twenty of my men and followed it for eight days and finnalt Came up with them in Camp on the Leona river about 30 miles from Fort Inge(south). We charged the camp and killed 7 of them which lay on the ground and wounded several others, we also Captured 4 head of horses three shields, 6 quivers with Bows and arrows, 2 Rifle guns and one Government revolver. We made various scouts too numerous to report, but all of which came off with success.

I Remain, Sir,
Your obt Servant
John M Davenport
Capt M M Volunteers

Indian raids increased slowly during 1857, but conditions on the frontier were critical enough for the legislature to approve a joint resolution authorizing the governor to raise "and muster in to the service of the state Mounted Men for the protection of our frontier." Under this resolution, approved November 17, 1857, Pease sent letters to Thomas C. Frost, John H. Conner and John Seaborn Hodges, all of whom had either formed detachments or been elected commander of new units.[4] These letters gave Conner a thirty-man detachment; Frost and Hodges were limited to twenty men each.

Governor Pease sent each officer instructions that differed from earlier commissions and authorizations. Along with his commission, Frost was cautioned not to interfere with reservation Indians unless he found them raiding. He was to act defensively, not making long scouts unless actually trailing a war party. Although he was allowed twenty rangers, only those actually required for security in his region were to be on duty.[5] For the first time, the settled Indians and the problems they had created were officially noticed, but trying to distinguish between Comanche raiders and the Indians on the reservations was often difficult. More and more settlers were unwilling even to try.

John Conner formed his small company in quick order at San Saba and was in the field by early December 1857. His initial report to the governor gives an unromanticized idea of life on the frontier during those harsh days. In novels and on the screen, almost every shot fired drops an enemy, horses never tire, men were fearless with keen eyesight, and rangers, especially, never missed their marks. As Captain Conner describes a few days, however, life was not that simple.

> Camp Colorado Decem 11.th 1857
> To Your excellency, E. M. Pease
>   Sir After mustering my company at San Saba - I
> went directly to Mr. Mercers- for the purpose of mus-
> tering in the men - On my arrival I was informed that
> he had gone to New Orleans - & that the citizens had
> sent to you for athority to raze a company in the place
> of Mr. Mercer - & wanted me to remain to muster
> them in. But I did not do so - as I could not have my
> own company. On my way from Mercers neighbor-
> hood, I stoped at a Mr. Johnsons on camp creek the
> only house from Mercers to Pecan Bayo - Mr.
> Johnson informed me that there was a company of
> Caddo Indians near him hunting - After travelling
> some six miles from Johnsons - Myself & the two
> men with- I discovered some men driving a cavyyard
> of horses leisurly along - just before me - whom I
> supposed to be white men - they were leaving the
> rode - & I was desirous of ascertaining the distance to
> Pecan Bayo - I put my horse in a gallop - & gallopped
> some hundred yards - When I discovered them to be
> Comanchy Indians - they left the Cavyyard & came
> gallopping up lesiurely to meet me - I still supposed
> them to Caddoes-as I had just bin informed that they
> were in the settlement - One of them had on hat -

when within a hundred yards- they hallowed friend
But still continued to advance - when within about
seventy yard - they razed the war hoop -& both razed
there bows to shoot one of them shot my horse in
the neck - which caused him to pitch & throw me off
- hurting my arm & shoulder conciderably - they
immediately charged the two men who were with me
- wounding one - & also his horse so soon as I could
get to my feet I drew my six shooter & shot at one
without doing any execution - the man who was still
unhurt I ordered to dismount - which he did shooting several times without doing any execution as they
had got some distance - My Horse that was wounded
& one of the other mens horses - ran of some three
hundred yards - the Indians pursued them - One of
them roped my horse - & the horse from the loss of
blood was so weak that he could not travel- the
Indians dismounted & stripped off all the riggings I
ordered William who was the well man to go down &
give them a fire - I had the wounded man in my
charge - we were making for the horses as fast as we
could. On discovering Williams who was in the
advance coming - they left my horse & rigging - One
of them springing on Williams horse which had got
away from him - Williams discharged his gun at him -
at the crack of which he fell dropping a buffalo robe
that he had with him - the other came running back
& assisted him on - they then made of with the cavy-
yard - carring Williams horse with them, & leaving
three of theirs - which ran off and was got by the
neighbors the next day. We were unable to pursue
them for want of horses those left us being wounded
& unable to travel - On arriving at Pecan Bayo that
night, - I learned that they Indians had bin in pursuit
of some white men - getting the hat from of them -
that he had on driving them from their work, they
stole some twelve horses at & with in some two miles
chandlers that day - On the fourth inst they killed a

calf with in one mile of new Camp Colorado I started
a company of men this morning - upon Pecan Bayo -
as high as the narrows - Also another with myself
down to the mouth of Pecan - sevral familyes have
recently moved up on the Concho & are begging for
protection - the citizens of Old Camp Colorado beg
that I would stay among them - the citizens all up and
down Pecan Bayo - are begging for protection. I want
you to let me have those other ten men - as I need
them much - I send you these lines by express hope-
ing to hear from you soon-I remain

Your Obt. Servant
Most Respectfully
John. H. Conner

P. S. In the skirmish I lost my muster roll- You will
be so kind as to forward me one coppy - also some of
the blanks - I want you to inform me if the reserve
Indians have a right to come down in the settlements
hunting - the people are complaining.[6]

The other detachments formed by Pease also made early reports,
although they were reporting to a new governor.[7] Lieutenant Thomas
C. Frost told of his early scouts in his area, paying particular attention
to a natural terrain corridor leading into the region. They tried to
catch a raiding band that came through the eastern part of Comanche
County and killed several people, stolen horses, captured two prisoners and then fled westward and north heading towards the reservations. Frost tried to be fair in his remarks, but he believed even if the
marauders were not reservation Indians, they were nevertheless
"friendly" natives.

Frost mentioned Major Neighbors had been petitioned time and
time again about real or suspected raids by Indians from the larger
reserve of settled tribes and the smaller reserve of Comanches. All
the citizens had received in reply had been threats, curses, denials and
renewed outrages. In closing, he outlined the difficulty of patrolling
a fifty-mile area with twenty men.[8]

At about the same time, Lieutenant John S. Hodges sent a brief
dispatch to Governor Runnels, reporting about the same results.

Although his twenty-man unit had been active, it was extremely difficult to catch Indians on foot. The raiders were seldom noticed until they stole horses or injured people or animals. He was after one group but had little hopes of finding them.[9]

During the latter days of 1857, Sergeant William B. Covington led a ranger detachment. G.H. Nelson commanded another group during October-December 1857, as will be seen, and Thomas K. Carmack raised and led a company from December 14, 1857, to March 14, 1858.[10]

None of the actions listed in reports of this period were large-scale battles; few even merited the term "skirmish," yet anything involving ball ammunition was serious. A raiding party of a dozen warriors was large. Most strikes were accomplished by a few men, often on foot, and even attacks by individuals were not unknown. Their chief purpose was stealing horses, but the Comanches did not hesitate to attack settlers, kill stock or burn isolated buildings. This widely scattered raiding by small groups had much to do with the U.S. Army's belief that the Texans were magnifying their Indian problem. Sitting in their widely separated posts, the soldiers seldom saw an Indian—so they must not be there. This view did not change to any degree until 1871 when General Sherman was almost killed in an ambush.[11]

It was not just the random killing or the constant loss of stock and horses that brought on a feeling of dread along the frontier. The threat alone was almost enough to paralyze an area. Additionally, the steady loss of farm animals and horses could bring financial ruin upon settlers who normally existed on little or nothing. Irate complaints often mentioned that pursuit could not be started because there were no horses. When their anguish over lost relatives or friends is added, the fear and anger of the frontier settlers can be understood.

Trying to determine where or when the raids would take place was almost impossible. Certain times of the year were favored such as periods of full moons. There were known terrain corridors leading into the settlements, and these could be watched if there were troops or rangers available. For the most part, actions were taken after a raid, and chasing any raiding party was extremely difficult. Without the occasional ranger scout or patrols between camps, the entire frontier would have been depopulated. The Mounted Men type of ranger units had barely enough time to form and become acquainted with the terrain before their two or three-month tour was over. The only effective answer to raids was a long-term force, preferably a *permanent*, regimental-size command. By the late 1850s this solution was obvious, but there was no way to finance such a large body of rangers.

Each governor, in turn, therefore, did the best he could and formed ranger detachments and companies to combat each emergency.

An unusual example of a ranger unit enrolled for a specific emergency had nothing to do with Comanches. In October 1857 attacks on Mexican cart drivers on the San Antonio/Laredo Road became so severe that special efforts were made to stop the ambushes. This trouble had its origins in the growing ill will between the Hispanic and the other citizens in southern Texas. Some of the bad feelings arose from blaming all Hispanics for helping slaves escape across the Rio Grande. A great part of the trouble was economic. Frederick Olmstead noticed that most of the "Mexicans"[12] in San Antonio were engaged in the manufacture of carts or engaged in transportation between San Antonio and Mexico. They undoubtedly worked for cheaper wages than Anglo drivers, creating further ill will.

Armed and usually masked bands started attacking the freight trains, beginning what would become known as the Cart War. In short order the outlaw gangs killed some seventy-five Hispanic cart drivers. Soon they made no distinction between civilian and military trains, and the U.S. Army was forced to assign guards to guard military supplies hauled by Hispanic drivers.[13] Governor Pease formed a short-term ranger company commanded by Captain G.H. Nelson to combat the situation and provide protection.[14]

Although in service for only a short period, the company did some good work and the trains they guarded were not attacked. Nelson, in San Antonio at the time, explained to Pease about one train that was ambushed by bandits on November 21, 1857. The carts, with Hispanic drivers, were led by William Pyron, brother of the owner of the freight involved. Two drivers were killed. Nelson pointed out he had not been asked for an escort and that all the trains guarded by the rangers had reached their destination unharmed.[15] Nelson added that the Pyron train, along with other carts, had finally gone on to Lavaca *with* a ranger guard. His last communication, some days later, announced that the unit's time of service was up and most of his men had been discharged although a twenty-man detachment led by a lieutenant still had to return from guard duty.[16]

While Nelson evidently did some good work, his unit demonstrated again the shortcomings of a sixty-day ranger company. The unit's major importance is in being one of the earliest ranger companies formed for a purely police role, even though the cart attacks were eventually halted by civilian action. As long as the bandits robbed and killed only Hispanics and Mexicans, the Anglo communities tolerated them. Most of the attackers seemed to have been known, but it was only after they began indiscriminate robbery that posses went out and began lynching them.

Governor H.R. Runnels

—6—
SENIOR CAPTAIN
"RIP" FORD

I n his *Memoirs*, George Erath discussed conditions along the Texas frontier in 1857-1858. An experienced Indian fighter and ranger commander during the Texas Republic, Erath had gone into politics and been elected a state senator in a district which included many of the exposed frontier counties and where protection of his people was a primary concern. Erath was careful to make a distinction between agency Indians and Comanche raiders. The settled Indians on the Brazos Reserve were making good progress in farming and adapting to "civilization," but the Indian fighter-turned-senator pointed out this did not apply to the residents on the smaller Comanche Reserve some sixty miles west where fewer Comanches lived because most had returned north to their old lands and ways. From their camps north of the Red River small bands came into Texas, often on foot, primarily to steal horses. They did not hesitate, however, to kill any unarmed Texans they encountered.[1]

In his final months in office, and hoping to stop such attacks, Governor Pease attempted to form a large ranger unit by preparing a draft bill and sending it to various individuals for comment. The governor asked for two majors, as was customary in the U.S. Army's horse regiments.[2] The governor's intent was to have the federal government fund this regiment but, not surprisingly, nothing came of his effort.

H.R. Runnels defeated Sam Houston for governor and assumed office during a time of renewed Indian violence. He, like earlier governors, appealed to the United States Congress for help,[3] but his appeal had the same result as earlier calls for aid and Runnels decided the state would have to look after itself.

Barely into another year, the new governor decided on a fresh approach. In a letter to the Texas Senate, Runnels outlined the situation in Texas. From all the evidence in his possession, he was satisfied there was a real and immediate danger from Indian raids. He stated that the four ranger detachments formed by Pease were inadequate to cover the borders, but raising the proper-sized force was difficult and responsibility rested with the legislature. He stressed it was the duty of the federal government to defend them; the state should not have this expense. Due to the extent of the frontier, a permanent force of several hundred men would be required. Lacking a large permanent force, a change of strategy was required and an expedition should be authorized to follow the Comanches to their distant hunting grounds and camps and punish them.[4] The Texas Legislature finally decided to do what was indicated and passed an Act for the Better Protection of the Frontier on January 27, 1858. Passive patrolling and retaliation was at an end; the rangers were to go north into Comanche territory.

Erath, who was largely responsible for the passage of the legislation, was praised in the press for his role.[5] The state senator explained some of the thinking behind the act he had fought so hard to pass: it was not intended so much to furnish frontier protection as it was to instigate an action with the Comanches and give notice to the federal government of its neglect in not protecting Texas.[6]

Runnels selected John Ford, "Rip" to friends, as commander of the new expedition, with the title of senior captain. In this dual capacity, he commanded all state troops.[7] On the same day as the appointment, January 28, 1858, the governor sent Ford a lengthy letter outlining his duties and responsibilities. Despite much verbiage, in modern military terminology Runnels issued a mission-type order.

> I impress upon you the necessity of action and energy. Follow any and all trails of hostile or suspected hostile Indians you may discover, and if possible overtake and chastise them if unfriendly.

Continuing, the governor stressed the necessity of cooperation between rangers, army, and Indian agents as essential to the protection of the frontier. Ford was to work with the army and coordinate his actions where possible. At the same time, Ford was not to submit to any interference with his duties. Runnels gave Ford authority to contract for needed supplies, saying he would approve such contracts. Finally, Ford was "clothed with the full and complete command of all State Troops, now in the service, and all to be called out..." Any and all officers now in service or elected in accordance with the Law of January 28, 1858, would be under Ford's command until otherwise directed by the governor.[8]

The earlier feelings of ill will against Ford following the Carbajal fiasco had long since faded, and his selection was popular. The news was greeted by editorial approval in Austin, where the new senior captain was commended and the United States castigated for not defending the frontier, forcing Texas to assume this task.[9]

Once again a ranger captain, Ford wasted no time entering active duty. He placed his name on the muster roll the same day he received his commission and orders, January 28, 1858. By February 5 he had fifty-seven men enrolled. Ed Burleson was back as senior lieutenant and quartermaster, with William A. Pitts as another lieutenant.[10] On February 8, Ford sent Burleson from Austin to San Antonio to buy mules and saddles and take over any property left from the mustering out of Nelson's detachment.[11]

Ford had decided on a camp location about twenty-five miles from Fort Belknap and directed an Austin contractor to forward supplies to this location.[12] By February 13, Ford had enough men signed up to send a partial muster roll to the governor. He noted that no recruits from the counties above Austin had yet been received, but their names would be forwarded without delay.[13]

When all the names were in, Ford had a company with 108 privates, four lieutenants, four sergeants, four corporals and two buglers. A sizable part of the new company came from the men of the ranger detachment in Bosque County, commanded by Allison Nelson, most of whom transferred to the new company. Nelson became one of the four lieutenants.[14]

Under his authority as senior captain, Ford disbanded the detachments commanded by Conner and Frost, the first on March 2 and Frost's on March 21. He mentions the termination of these detachments in his *Memoirs*, but with scant explanation other than to wonder if he had ill treated Frost.[15] He explained to the governor, however, that at the time he supposed the units formed by Pease would automatically be mustered out when their three months was finished.[16]

Ford had not waited in Austin until his new command was ready; he started north and west late in February.[17] From an initial report, it seems the date was February 27, 1858.[18] In this letter to Governor Runnels, Ford outlined the first stage of his campaign: a parallel sweep by four detachments of his company to search for mounted Indians. He was satisfied there were no Indians on horseback, although there were signs of foot Indians. On this part of the campaign, Ford used Lieutenant Frost's detachment as one part of his thrust. He also pulled in Lieutenant Nelson's rangers from Bosque County and used them as another part of the scout. When this stage was finished, Ford sent Nelson and the men who had transferred to the camp near Belknap. During this time Ford met with Major Earl Van Dorn, the senior U.S. Army officer in the region.

Ford reported again on March 31 after reaching their camp, which they named Camp Runnels in honor of the governor.[19] He again summarized actions, including reports from Burleson and Pitts.[20] Both officers had chased Comanche bands, driving them back north but never catching up for a fight. Ford had visited the Brazos Agency and found Agent Shapley P. Ross eager to cooperate in a campaign against the Comanches. The Plains Indians had declared war on the agency Indians, and the more settled tribes were eager for a fight. All agreed the only solution to stopping raids was to move up and attack the Comanche on their hunting grounds. Ford had been worried about a campaign so far north with only a hundred rangers, but the promise of at least a hundred Indian allies changed his thinking. "When we take up the line of march we shall feel assured of being able to direct our course upon the Comanche camp. I am now sanguine of success."

In an age when commanders are in immediate touch with headquarters half a world away, it is interesting to note Ford mentioned he had no reply to his March 11 report. Also, he had not seen the two rangers he left in Austin to forward messages. The weather had been bad, with high water and impassable roads. Despite this, the Texas Secretary of State had Ford's March 31 report and replied for the absent governor by April 8, a commendable effort for the courier service of the day.[21]

Although Ford was naturally concerned about his immediate mission as commander of the major force to fight the Comanches, Texans further south had their own problems. Citizens in San Saba and adjoining counties petitioned Runnels to recognize a volunteer company they had formed. D.C. Cowan had written earlier, and on March 5 he wrote T.S. Anderson, Secretary of State, another letter [mis]spelling out briefly and bluntly that "I can further assure you and the governor that this request is from your political friend and as far as known personal allso, pleas answer immediately."[22]

Whether politics or the actual need most influenced Runnels is unknown—perhaps a little of each. Whatever his motivation, he wrote John Williams and authorized him to form a twenty-man detachment. The men were to furnish everything: horses, saddles, a good rifle or shot gun, one or more pistols and ammunition. The rangers would look to the legislature for pay which, if allowed, would be the same as other troops in service. They were to serve for sixty days.[23] The same day Cowan sent his letter, John Conner wrote requesting another company.[24] Nothing came of this request.

Up north, Ford had more than enough to occupy him. As he had before, Ford spent considerable time drilling his rangers, especially firing at targets from horseback. At the same time, a close watch was kept on the agency Indians.[25] Recruiting the agency Indians was the task of Shapley Ross, who spent much time and used his extensive knowledge of Indian customs to convince his charges it was right to fight their old enemy, the Comanche.[26] One day there was a great war dance on the reserve, witnessed by all the Indians and invited ranger guests,[27] and Ford finally obtained his hundred Indian volunteers.

In view of what happened to these reservation Indians a short time later, it seems proper that at least their leaders should be remembered. No muster rolls are preserved in the state archives listing all their names; a few of the leaders are known and are hereby saluted.

Jim Pockmark, leader of the Caddos and Anadarkos, and Jose Casa Maria, second chief.

Placido, chief of the Tonkawas, and O'Quinn, a Tonk war captain.

Shot Arm, chief of the Wacos.

Jim Linney, captain of the Shawnees and Delawares.
Nid-e-wats, captain of the Tahuacanos.
Keechi, chief spy, with Caddo John, Chul-e-quah and Jem Logan.

While final preparations were being made, Ed Burleson was called back to the settlements to attend to critical personal business. After so much work and effort, he would miss the final struggle.[28] In an interesting feature of the last days of preparation for the push beyond the Red River, Agent Ross brought in a minister to speak to the Indians. Reverend Tackett spoke through Jim Shaw, an interpreter. It was evidently a hell-fire, frontier sermon because the Indians were greatly impressed and later credited the "medicine man" with winning their victory![29] Other preparations were more mundane: checking rations, preparing ammunition, storing supplies in two wagons, and helping Doctor Powhatan Jordan collect what medical supplies were available. There was no corn for the horses, and the animals would have to do with grass. Food supplies were adequate with plenty of flour, coffee and sugar. Bacon was not plentiful, but they expected to obtain meat by hunting.[30]

A late arrival was Captain William Ford, father of the commander, driving a light wagon which was taken along to carry any wounded. Ford made no effort to talk his father out of going along; the elder Ford was a young seventy-three and as tough as any ranger in the force.[31]

On April 22, 1858, everything was in place and the rangers headed north. The story of the last weeks of the campaign has been told before, but never better than in Ford's report.[32]

> Head Quarters Texas Rangers
> Camp Runnels May 22nd 1858
> Gov
> I have the honor to report, that on the 22nd of April I made a forward movement from this Camp at the head of one hundred and two men, including officers, non-commissioned officers, privates and guides, I also had two waggons one Ambulance and fifteen pack mules.
> At the Cottonwood Springs I was joined by Capt

S.P. Ross, and one hundred and thirteen Indians of
the Brazos Reservation. We directed our March upon
Red River—reaching and crossing that stream on the
29th. The Command marched up the valley of the
river, made frequent halts, and sent out spies and
detachments to make frequent reconnoisances of the
surrounding Country. This plan of operations was
continued until the 7 of May without discovery of
any very recent Indian sign. We then determined to
march in the direction of the Wachita River—A
Branch of which was reached on the 8th of May. Our
spies reported a large trail leading down the country.
We followed it for two days. On the evening of the
10th the spies brought in a couple of Comanche
arrow-heads, extracted from a buffalo found
wounded, which they killed. Convinced that we were
now in the vicinity of a large body of the enemys
every precaution was taken to avoid being decovered
[*sic*] and every possible exertion made to find their
Camp. Had we succeeded in the latter we should have
moved near it in the night, and just before day-light
sent in a party of our Indians to stampede the horses
and we should have attacked the enemy immediately.
On the 11th the spies reported having seen
Comanches running buffalo, and they likewise had
gotten a correct notion of the course to their camp
by watching pack animals as they transported buffalo
meat to it. I prepared to move upon the enemy without delay. I left a small guard at my camp, and at 2
O'Clock P.M. marched with one hundred Americans
and Capt Ross' command of one hundred and thirteen friendly Indians. When we reached the Fort
Smith and Sante Fe road we saw Comanches moving
about in the valley beyond the "divide," apparently
unconscious of our proximity. When they had gone
we resumed our March—Confining our selves to the
low grounds and ravines to keep out of sight. We
halted at dusk, camped and sent forward some

Indians to overtake our Keechi Spy and trailer. Unfortunately they missed him and he remained out side of camp until day light, on the morning of the 12th, when he joined us on the march. Our plan was frustrated, and we were compelled to march upon the foe in open day. The pursuit was made most of the time at a gallop. At 7 O Clock A.M. a small camp of five Lodges was discovered and taken. The Toncahua Indians remained, demolished the camp, took some prisoners, and mounted their foot-men. Two Comanches fled towards the Canadian and were followed by the whole command at nearly full speed. After a run of three miles a large encampment was visible from a hill top, about three miles distant, and on the Cherokee side of the Canadian. We saw the two Comanches passing the river and followed at a run—crossing the stream without holding up—and reached the camp just after they had given the alarm. Capt. Ross led his Indians between the Lodges and the river, and they engaged the enemy. I halted for a moment for my men to come up and then gave the order to charge the camp, which was executed promptly and gallantly. The Comanches intended to have made a stand at this point—the Rangers pressed them closely and they fled in every direction. The right wing in charge of myself and Lt William A. Pitts, moved straight through the camp and poured in a galling fire upon the retreating enemy. Lt Allison Nelson in command of the Left wing, assisted by Lt James H. Tankersley and Lt Wm G Preston, charged to the left and pursued the flying Comanches with vigor—and effect. In the meantime the head chief, Iron Jacket, had ridden out in gorgeous array—clad in a coat of mail—and bore down upon our red allies. He was followed by warriors and trusted for safty [sic] to his armor. The sharp crack of five or six rifles brought his horse to the ground, and in a few moments the Chief fell riddled with balls. Our

Shawnee guide, Doss, and Jim Pockmark, the
Anodarco Captain, claim the first and last wounds.
The fight was now general, and extended, very soon,
over a circuit of six miles in Length and more than
three in breadth. It was in fact, almost, a series of single combats. Squads of Rangers and Indians were
pursuing the enemy in every direction. The
Comanches would occasionally halt and endeavor to
make a stand, however, their efforts were unavailing -
they were forced to yield the ground to our men in
every instance. The din of battle had rolled back from
the river—the groans of the dying, cries of frightened women and children, mingled with the reports
of firearms, and the shouts of the men as th[e]y rose
from Hill top, from thicket, and from ravine.

The second chief had rushed into the conflict
with the friendly Indians. A shot from the Shawnee
Captain, Chul-le-qua, closed his career. The
Comanches between the Camp and the river were all
killed and driven from the field, and our red allies sent
up a wile shout of triumph. By direction of Capt
Ross a portion of them held the camp of the enemy.

The Rangers and the friendly Indians still pressed
the Comanches, nor did they stop pursuing until their
failing horses admonished them, that they could do
no more. Between twelve and one O'clock the firing
had almost ceased; and squad after squad of our
troups were returning to the Comanche Camp, bringing with them horses prisoners and other trophies of
victory. Capt Ross had very properly suggested to Lt
Nelson the propriety of keeping the men well
together, and when I returned from the pursuit I
found a large proportion of the men drawn up in
order of battle.

The Comanches had another large encampment
three or four miles above on the Canadian. They had
heard the firing, embodied, and threatened to charge
us. They were evidentally playing for an advantage

and their manoeuvreres [*sic*] induced our Indians to
believe them very strong. Our allies proposed to draw
them out, and requested me to keep my men in line to
support them, if necessary. The Commanches
descended from the hill to accept their profered invi-
tation. With yells, and menaces, and every species of
insulting gesture, and language, they tried to excite the
Reserve Indians into some act of rashness by which
they could profit. A scene was now enacted beggaring
description. It reminded one of the rude and chivalrous days of Knight-errantry. Shields and Lances, and
bows, and head dresses—prancing steeds and many
minutias were not wanting to compile the resem-
blance. And when the combatants rushed at each
other with defiant shouts, nothing save the piercing
report of the rifle, varied the affair from the battle
field of the middle ages. Half an hour was spent in
this without much damage to either party. A detachment of Rangers was advanced to reinforce the
friendly Indians, and the Comanches quited the field,
and the imposing pagent vanished from the view like
a mimic battle upon the stage.

It was determined to leave the Indians in possession of the prisoners and captured horses, and to hurl
the Rangers upon the Comanches. My men made a
forward movement, if not with the precision of practiced veterans, yet with as much coolness and bravery.
The enemy instantly began the retreat. I directed Lt
Pitts to show him self and detachment upon the hill
with the intention to steal upon them. Lt Nelson
anticipated me and passed around the base of the
eminence at a run. The unfortunate arrival of the
Toncahua Indians upon our left flank prevented the
complete success of the maneouvre. The Comanches
broke and fled in various directions. We pursued as
fast as our jaded horses could carry us. After a run of
two and a half or three miles I saw we could effect no
more and called off the men. In this second conflict

the enemy lost seven killed and left on the ground, and a number were wounded. Our loss was one Waco Indian killed and one Ranger [one word blotted] wounded, [George W. Paschal Jr.] [33] It was now 2 O Clock P.M. and we had been running our horses much of the time since 7 Oclock A.M. I determined to march to my camp that night—fearing the Indians might ascertain its locality and over-power the weak guard left to protect it. We learned from a captured woman that Buffalo Hump was twelve miles below us with a considerable body of warriors, and we knew fugitives had reached his camp and notified him of our presence. The forces of the enemy in these two engagements amounted to upwards of three hundred—The captured camp had seventy lodges and fires; The other party numbered over one hundred

Our entire force was two hundred and thirteen The loss of the enemy, ascertained by actual count, of those remaining on the field, was as followes

First Engagement - Killed 69
Second   "   "   7

Total 76

Our Loss
First Engagement - Killed 1   Wounded 2
Second   "   - Killed 1   "   1

2   3

The enemy had many wounded, but it was impossible to ascertain the number, and therefore no guess will be made. We captured over three hundred head of horses—most of them are in the possession of the friendly Indians; some fifty or sixty are in the hands of my men. There are few if any American horses among them. We took eighteen prisoners, mostly women and children.

For further particulars in regard to the operation of the Left wing I beg leave to refer you to the report of Lt A Nelson.

A Mexican boy was taken prisoner, and told a Mexican Muleteer, that the Comanches were drying and packing meat to make a campaign against the whites and Reserve Indians. It may not be true, though the bales of dry meat were there to show for them selves. The Mexican escaped the night of the twel[f]th.

I am under weighty obligations to Capt S. P. Ross for his valuable advice and cordial co-operation during the expedition. He did much to render it successfully. I beg leave to recommend to your favorable notice Lts Nelson, Tankersly, and Preston. They performed their respective duties promptly cheerfully and ably. The conduct of the men of my command was characterized by obedience patience and perseverance. They behaved, while under fire in a gallant and soldier like manner and I think that they have fully vindicated their right to be recognized as Texas Rangers of the old stamp. I could point out many instances of chivalrous daring on their part during the engagements, but where all have done their parts well, nobly well, distinctions would be invidious. In justice to our Indian allies I beg leave to say they acted their part with zeal and fidelity; and they behaved most excellently on the field of battle. They deserve well of Texas and are entitled to the gratitude of the frontier people.

About 2 O Clock P.M. we took up the line of march for camp. In a little while signal smokes of the Comanches were shooting up from different quarters. They indicated flight. Our horses were worn down by service, our rations of meat had been exhausted several days, and there appeared but little prospect of effecting any thing by remaining longer; there fore, it was decided to leave on the morning of the 13th for Camp Ruinnels, which we reached on the 21st after an absence of thirty days.

Accompanying is a map defining our line of march. This expedition has decided several questions—Indians can be pursued and caught in the Buffalo region—the country beyond Red river can be penetrated and held by white men, and the Comanches can be followed, overtaken, and beaten, providing the pursuers will be laborious vigilant, and are willing to undergo privations.

The two waggons and ambulance were broken down and abandoned on the home march. They answered a valuable purpose. I am at a loss to know what to do and am awaiting orders

> I have the honor to be your Obt Servt
> John S. Ford
> Capt. Commanding
> Texas Frontier.

Ford's report reached Austin in less than a week, because Governor Runnels acknowledged receipt of the victory message and congratulated the ranger on May 28, 1858.[34] In his reply, the governor sensibly turned back the question of what the ranger should do; Ford was on the ground and the best judge of future actions. Runnels gave him authority to call out more men, if necessary, and to make another campaign. He was, however, to leave behind enough men to protect the settlements.

In addition to the personal message to Ford, Runnels dispatched an address to the members of the expedition. It was noteworthy for its specific mention of the Indians from the Brazos Reservation, giving them equal glory for the recent victory.[35]

Despite his detailed report, Ford did not mention specifics about his own loss, slight as it was, but many years later he recounted the story of the one ranger death. When the Comanches were routed in the first engagement, the rangers and the reservation Indians pursued them, usually in small groups. Rangers Oliver Searcy and Robert Nickles were separated from their squad and considerably in advance of the rest of the command. Out front and alone, they ran onto a body of Comanches coming to reinforce the fleeing Indians. Searcy, an experienced fighter, told his companion to turn about and fire from time to time, threatening the enemy and keeping them at a distance until they could rejoin the main body or escape among the many ravines in the area. Either Nickles did not hear or his horse bolted, because he rode right into a party of Comanches who killed him with their lances. Searcy fell back, turning to fire whenever one of the Indians came too close. He finally abandoned his horse and hid in a ravine until some of the other rangers rode up and rescued him.[36]

When the friendly Indians reached the Brazos Reserve, the women and children, alerted to their victorious return, greeted them with cries of joy. Dressed in their best garments, they welcomed the returning heroes with wild yells and dancing. The warriors, carrying captured shields and lances, bows and quivers, and driving over two-hundred horses, rode up as victorious armies have done since earliest days. It was time to celebrate a great win over their traditional enemies the Comanche, much booty, and almost no casualties. The sixty Comanche women and children captives were divided among the other tribes or allowed to settle where they wished on the reservation.[37]

The rangers went into camp at Camp Runnels. A few days after his arrival, Ford reported again to the governor and outlined his plans for the future: first he had to rest his horses; then he proposed dividing his force to defend exposed areas in the vicinity. He planned to scout the upper Colorado as well as scour the San Saba. He was sending out spies to locate any large Comanche bands, but he ruled out another expedition, at least until fall.

Ford was well aware of the political forces involved in raising ranger units and mentioned the expedition had been a success, thus saving Runnels from embarrassment. Once more, Ford stressed his company was not strong enough to defend the frontier unaided; only the proposed permanent regiment could do this job. Until such a force was raised, the piecemeal companies and detachments were actually frittering away public money.[38]

For the time being, however, small detachments had to do the job. John Williams' twenty-man detachment, formed in May, had been active but made no newspaper headlines as had Ford. Williams reported that he split his unit into two groups and scouted each day, hoping to pick up signs of raiders. People in his area were frightened the Comanches might try revenge raids following Ford's victory. He was busy, going as far west as the old stone fort on the San Saba River. Williams asked the governor to remember him if the regiment was formed. He noted his men had spent more money getting ready than they would receive from the state, but if they kept Indians from stealing or killing on the frontier they were satisfied.[39]

In addition, Runnels had raised a company in June, commanded by William Marlin, to protect the Brazos Agency. Ford re-mustered these rangers, about twenty-five in number, when he set up Camp Runnels. They were to cover the country between the two Indian agencies.[40] Much later, on October 28, Colonel James Bourland led a company organized to scout between the Trinity and the Red River.[41]

There was a calm period following the severe defeat of the Comanches, and Ford's company was discharged on August 5, 1858.[42] The Comanches were not a single tribe, led by a hereditary chief, but a collection of several distinct bands each led by a chief. These chiefs changed from time to time, and every war band or raiding party had a leader chosen for the occasion. Ford had not shattered the Comanche Nation; he had merely defeated one part of one band. They fled to safer ground, selected new leaders and came back. Towards the end of 1858, repeated calls for help forced Runnels to ask Ford once again to form a ranger company.[43]

As directed, Ford formed his new company in Austin. Although he had been designated to head the unit, Ford went through the formality of being elected on November 4, 1858, to rank from November 12.[44] He evidently had little doubt about being elected— he signed a contract for rations the day before the vote![45] The new command was mustered into service on November 10, 1858.[46] This company, largely composed of young men, started for the frontier in two detachments, again to the praise and high hopes of editors and friends.[47]

The muster rolls of Ford's two companies show a marked change in the arming of rangers compared to several years earlier. During the service in south Texas in 1849-1850, few rangers had revolvers. By 1855, when Callahan made his raid, muster rolls and claims for lost weapons show considerable numbers and models of revolvers, but also some old pistols. In 1858, only an occasional ranger did not have

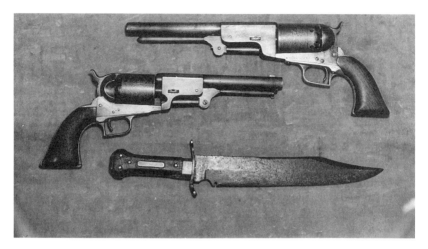

Ranger weapons. During the early years of this period, Texas Rangers used whatever weapons were available. For a time, they were not armed as well as they were in the later days of the Republic, or during the Mexican War. In addition to old Army, single-shot muzzle-loading pistols, they used an occasional "Walker" Colt (top), or the more recent Colt "Dragoon" model (middle). Every Ranger had some form of belt knife, although the example displayed here is not typical of the period. *Courtesy of The Texas Ranger Hall of Fame, Waco.*

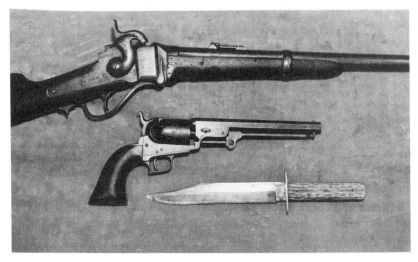

Ranger weapons. The favorite Ranger arms of the late 1850s. Sharps breech-loading carbine (top), Colt .36 caliber revolver, the "Navy" (center), and a typical belt knife (bottom). *Courtesy of The Texas Ranger Hall of Fame, Waco.*

one of the new Colts. The first rangers had tested and proved the five-shot Colt revolvers, and now these latter-day fighters eagerly accepted the new revolvers, especially the so-called Navy Model of 1851. It took some time for these arms to reach the frontier in large numbers. When Frederick Olmstead traveled through Texas in 1853, he commented on the use of Colt revolvers and the new Sharps breech-loading rifle and carbine.[48] His remarks would suggest that everyone had these improved weapons, but this was far from the case; the average settler did not have the thirty-five dollars or more to pay for a revolver or rifle. The rangers were able to afford them because of their pay—*if* they were paid. In many cases, weapons were furnished and the cost deducted from their final settlement.

However obtained, Ford's rangers were well armed when they started north. They made a base camp in Comanche County with a stockade enclosure, guard house, and a building to store their supplies. With new men mostly unfamiliar with frontier living, Ford spent some time drilling and shaping his company. This was not to be a repeat of the glory days in April and May. There was only one alert, after which the rangers started out on a fresh trail. The Indians had stolen horses and managed to escape Ford, but Lieutenant Williams and his Minute Men overtook and scattered the band.[49]

The remainder of their service consisted of endless scouting in an effort to locate a sizable Comanche camp. Ford considered a joint expedition with the U.S. Army, but Major Earl Van Dorn, the senior officer, evidently had his own ideas and wanted no part of the "volunteers." The army regulars had complained to Shapley Ross about favoring the rangers, and the agent offered his services and the agency Indians for another expedition. Much the same band joined the expedition with units of the 2nd Cavalry. However, when Ross was ready to go, the Indian leaders begged him to stay, fearing he would be killed, and Lawrence S. Ross, his twenty-year-old son, led the Indians. In September Van Dorn led this mixed column and won another victory over a Comanche band north of the Red River. In the fight, Van Dorn and young Ross were severely wounded.[50] Great claims were made for this fight, including the belief the Comanches had been finally shattered, but the only real result was making "Sul" Ross a Texas hero and easing the way for his ranger career.

When Ford learned Van Dorn had left on his own expedition, he gave up any idea of cooperating with the army. He took part of his company and Indian guides and crossed the Red River, scouting as far north as the Pease. If they achieved nothing else, Ford saw new lands and became convinced it could be wheat-growing country. The fact that the Comanches spent the summer hunting buffalo here showed there was water and wood. Grass grew in profusion, why not wheat? The expedition exemplified the secondary benefits of ranger service, opening new trails and exploring and mapping country beyond the frontier line.

Only one incident on this scout is of more than incidental interest. Much later, Ford learned they had been very close to a large Comanche camp. His Indian scouts located the enemy and were frightened by the numbers opposing them. Knowing Ford would fight, whatever the odds, they returned and reported there was no water and they would have to turn back. Ford had some doubts but could see his allies would go no farther. The rangers were too few to fight; without the Indians, there could be no battle. He was bitterly disappointed, as he hoped to take advantage of the long-range accuracy of the new Minie Rifles just issued to his men. He believed he could stay well away from the Comanches and shoot them to bits.[51]

The rangers returned to the Comanche Agency, then over to the Brazos Agency where Lieutenant Marlin and his detachment were paid and mustered out, as were the Indian guides and scouts. Ford carried money for this purpose, but he did not have enough to settle the account for supplies bought by Marlin. The state of Texas probably still owes a contractor for that particular bill.[52]

Returning to their base camp, the rangers marched through Palo Pinto County, attracting considerable attention. Many settlers believed they had come to arrest some whites who had shot seven agency Indians, but Ford had no intention of meddling in what was developing into a semi-civil war. When their six months was up, the company was discharged. It had accomplished little of what was expected, and, with the seventy-thousand dollars set aside for this expedition depleted, no new effort or funds were expended to muster in another company. Ford mentioned many of the rangers retained their weapons, which were charged to them and probably never paid for. The remaining arms were turned in but were not properly collected nor receipts maintained, creating another squabble which lasting until 1860 when Ford was finally cleared of any financial liability.[53]

Ford's second expedition accomplished little, but the march back to his camp and his refusal to serve a warrant to arrest Peter Garland and others accused of killing agency Indians in Palo Pinto County did have some lasting implications. The controversy lasted for months, with accusations, counter-claims and defenses filling the newspapers until well into 1859. Ford has an entire section in his *Memoirs* devoted to this incident, explaining in great detail and some self-serving eloquence why he did not serve the writ to arrest Garland.[54]

Condensing the Garland matter into the necessary details, a party of whites had killed agency Indians, believing them to be responsible for hostile acts. It was part of the rapidly developing struggle between the frontier settlers and *all* Indians, Plains or settled, hostile or friendly. This act, however, was blatant enough for a judge to issue a warrant for the arrest of Garland and others implicated in the murders. The writ was sent to Ford for service. He refused, claiming the arrest would lead to a civil war between his rangers and the settlers. His polished explanation was attacked by an equally reasoned explanation why he *should* have served the writ, whatever the consequences. Even Runnels was involved, sending Ford a letter stressing his obligation to assist the civil authorities. Ford made a special point of the word "assist;" he was willing to *assist* but unwilling to take full responsibility.[55]

The claims and counter claims finally died out. The controversy seems almost childish now, with Ford clearly in the wrong, and nothing was clarified concerning the civil role of the rangers. Jack Hays had chased horse thieves during the Republic years, though not as a basic mission, and a detachment had been formed to try to stop the killings in the Cart War, certainly a civil mission, but Ford chose to consider himself and his rangers as a military force. They might back up the local sheriff, but they would not assume his duties. The question would arise again in later years when the rangers finally became a statewide police force. It is clear Governor Runnels saw them in this role in 1858.

The expeditions of Ford and Van Dorn were the dramatic events of 1858, even if they did not permanently halt Comanche raids; the

Indians could absorb two defeats and still return to their old games. The settlers along the Texas frontier continued to be threatened by raids, particularly during every full moon. By October petitions for help were arriving in Austin, and the governor was faced with the seemingly endless task of defending the settlements.

There was a sizable Indian raid in the San Saba/Lampasas region in October. John Williams' company followed the tracks of a raiding party and discovered the bodies, one severely mutilated, of four members of the Joshua Jackson family.[56] Two boys in the family escaped the attack, but two others were missing and believed captured. The rangers were forced to halt extensive tracking due to lack of supplies.[57] At least some of the Indians responsible for the attack on the Jackson family were caught by a volunteer patrol. They were Comanches; one was killed and two wounded. Many stolen horses were recovered. Clothing belonging to the Jacksons was abandoned by this band.[58]

Because of considerable Indian activity in Wise County, on October 4, 1858, Governor Runnels called on Colonel James Bourland to raise a company, as mentioned earlier. About all Runnels could do was promise to furnish ammunition; everything else, as usual, would depend on the legislature. Runnels told Bourland to cooperate with Van Dorn but to cross the Red River if necessary, and if there appeared a chance of success. In a note to his original message, Runnels instructed Bourland to wait until it was absolutely necessary to form the company. He promised to send instructions.[59]

Bourland finally was able to form his company on December 28, 1858, serving until January 28, 1859, when his term of service was extended until April 28, 1859.[60]

Although a considerable numbers of reservation Indians had fought gallantly with Ford and Van Horn, many settlers blamed them for the raids that resumed in the closing months of 1858. It was common for friendly Indians to hunt off reservation land where they were familiar sights to Texans in the area, but many of the people in George Erath's district were recent arrivals in Texas and could not tell one Indian from another. The Comanches slipped in on foot and stole horses and often returned on trails that led directly towards the Brazos Reserve, a tactic Lieutenant Frost had mentioned earlier in an effort to be fair to friendly Indians. The situation became increasingly volatile.

During Christmas of 1858 a twenty-man posse, largely composed of newcomers to the area, found a party of Brazos Indians about fifteen miles outside the reservation and opened fire, killing several Indians. Returning fire, the Indians shot and killed a sixteen-year-old boy. News of the fight traveled quickly, and three-hundred men assembled and elected Allison Nelson their commander. In the time since he had been a lieutenant with Ford, a considerable change had taken place in their relationship; they had fallen out when the lieutenant supposedly proposed laying a false trail to the Comanche Reserve and thereby giving an excuse to attack them. The situation was further acerbated by the hate of John Baylor, one of the Indian Agents, for Supervising Agent Neighbors, whom he attempted to have removed. Baylor apparently offered Neighbors' agency position to Nelson, who was at least interested. Ford, in later years, mentions there was a disagreement but claimed to have forgotten the cause. The trouble was taken to Washington, and a federal investigation cleared Neighbors.[61]

Whatever his ambitions, Nelson realized the explosive potential of the situation and tried to distance himself as a participant. He wrote Erath, advising him of the brewing trouble. Ex-ranger Erath rode to the settler camp and found the Texans were not just considering fighting Indians but were even ready to shoot it out with the soldiers guarding the reservation! With their state senator in camp, the men agreed to wait and chose Erath and two others to talk with Indian leaders and the army officers on the reservation, but Erath recalled that "More or less was said to little purpose." The senator explained to the Indians that the Texans demanded they stay on the reservation and leave Texas as soon as possible. He believed they were not excited, either agreeing to go or already resigned to expulsion. Returning to the camp of the settlers, he found they were willing to listen even if no firm agreement had been signed. Most people near the reservations were opposed to vigilante action. The bulk of Nelson's old command came from nearby counties and shortly returned to their homes, leaving matters in a state passing for peace.

Although a disruption of chronology, it is convenient here to follow the sad tale of the reservation Indians. There was no major disruption of the peace until the spring of 1859 when a raiding band swept over a hundred miles through the frontier settlements. They collected a large herd of stolen horses and killed a man and his wife about twenty miles from Belton, far inside the frontier zone. They returned north unchecked. There were no more discussions, nor were there any distinctions made between reservation Indians and wild Comanches when volunteers and scouts located some reservation Indians outside the reservation boundary. Over five-hundred angry men gathered below the Brazos Reservation. Alarmed at this assembly, Erath sent a special messenger to Governor Runnels.[62]

Runnels sent an express to the volunteer camp informing them he was appointing a Board of Commissioners to come to the camp and discuss the difficulty. He specifically stated he was trying to avoid the shedding of blood or an open fight with U.S. troops. He promised a definite solution to the trouble and the expulsion of the Indians.[63] The same day on which he wrote Nelson and the settlers, the governor sent instructions to the men selected as commissioners: J.M. Steiner, John Henry Brown, Richard Coke, James Smith and George Erath.[64] Runnels stressed their first mission was to prevent conflicts between Indians and the citizens of Texas. They were to meet with all parties. He cautioned them about taking sides and warned them to leave past conflicts to the courts. They were, however, to gather any facts that might be used by the courts to determine guilt. He made it clear the commissioners were to cooperate with the Indian agents, the commanding officers of U.S. forces and the local citizens in maintaining the peace. They were to urge the citizen volunteers to return home and the Indians to remain on their reservations. If talk did not suffice, commissioners could call out ranger-type companies of up to one-hundred men.

By the time the commissioners reached the Brazos Reservation and began talks with Captain J.B. Plummer, the commander of the troops guarding the Indians, most of the volunteers had returned home. Unfortunately, the hundred or so who remained had managed to create another dangerous confrontation when some of them entered the reservation and engaged in a shouting match with Plummer and some Indians. When they started to leave, the angry Indians opened fire, killing one settler and wounding others.

Despite the incident, Erath and the commissioners started their work, and the senator praised the captain for his courteous treatment. Neighbors was absent on business, but Agent Shapley Ross was present and defended his Indians in a vigorous manner. He told the commissioners that arrangements had been made to move the Indians in August. All that remained was obtaining necessary transport and collecting supplies, equipment and Indian stock.[65]

With the assurance that the Indians would be removed to north of the Red River, the most troublesome of the commissioners' duties was resolved, but the situation was still extremely delicate. Much ill will had developed as a result of the claims and counter claims of Baylor and Neighbors. Ross' strong defense of his agency Indians had not made him any friends along the frontier. Erath and the other commissioners visited county seats in the area, explaining the situation and trying to calm the settlers. Observing the general unrest, the commissioners took advantage of their vested authority and formed a ranger company in case there was more trouble. John Henry Brown was elected captain.[66]

Brown formed his company, with a mustering in date of June 28, 1859. He marched towards the Brazos Reservation and met or sent a message to Neighbors on July 12. When he arrived at Caddo Spring on July 14, he wrote Neighbors confirming his verbal message. He clearly outlined his instructions to prevent future violence, by either side, and offered his help to the agent in any way. Brown offered to provide guards for any agency Indians who needed to gather loose animals outside the reservation boundaries. It was a business-like, conciliatory message.[67]

Neighbors made no effort to accept help or cooperate in any way with the rangers. Fortunately, there was no trouble with the Brazos Indians, but the smaller group of Comanches, to the west on their own reserve, was another story. A sizable party of Comanches was discovered away from the reservation, and a fight developed between a ranger force, led by one of Brown's lieutenants, and the Indians. Details of the fight are few, but it occurred towards the end of July and the Comanches supposedly lost eleven warriors and were driven back onto the reservation. The rangers had two men wounded.[68] When the governor heard of the fight, he wrote and gave Brown his full support and approval.[69]

The fight did not slow or halt the plans for moving the Indians.

The departure from the Brazos Agency began on August 1, 1859, when a long caravan started for the Red River.[70] Two companies of the 2nd Cavalry and a company of the 1st Infantry, commanded by Major George H. Thomas, guarded the Indians. Neighbors completely ignored Brown's offer of help and did not even let Brown know the Indians were leaving; the rangers found out the next day and started after the column.

Despite the urgent need to move the column, Neighbors halted the march after a few miles to allow the agency personnel to vote in the state's gubernatorial election. How the agency employees voted is unknown, but there is little doubt the agency Indians and the entire perception of frontier safety played some part in Runnels' losing in his second race with Sam Houston. Their citizenship duties completed, Neighbors and his people continued the slow march north and reached the Red River on August 7. The Comanche Reservation column joined the others the same day, and the next day they all began the river crossing. From that day on, any Indian south of the Red River was considered to be hostile.

Brown and his company rode up, made camp on the Little Washita, and sent an express to Major Thomas stating that, because he had not been told when the Indians would be leaving, he should be allowed to examine any animals brought north by the Indians. Brown received scant satisfaction from the officer, who informed him no Indians had left the march and the citizens were satisfied no cattle had been carried away.[71] Just how Thomas knew what the citizens thought is unclear.

After he returned to his camp at Caddo Spring, Brown submitted a report on the move stating he had started after the agency Indian column on August 2 and had camped on the Little Washita. From this base, he scouted forty miles east and west and up to the Red River, finding the country generally unhealthy. Several of the rangers became sick and one died. Brown noted that on the march up, on August 4, part of his company was scouting and chased two Indian parties which Brown believed were agency Indians. The rangers recovered thirteen horses which Brown said had been stolen from citizens near the agency. Brown's claim is interesting in view of Thomas' statement that no Indians left the column. Brown stated he left the area on August 13 after all the Indians had crossed the Red River. He requested someone meet him in Waco and in Belton, where the two detachments in his company would be discharged.[72] All the rangers were mustered out by September 12, 1859.[73]

There is an equally unhappy ending to this unhappy story of the removal of the Indians from Texas. Major John Neighbors spent much of his life trying to solve the Indian problem in Texas. Many people respected him for what he had attempted and accomplished, even while acknowledging he was fighting for a hopeless cause, but others hated him and opposed everything he stood for. Shortly after Neighbors returned to Texas, an unknown assassin came up behind him in the town of Belknap and killed him. He was buried in an unmarked grave in the civilian cemetery.[74]

General Juan Cortina

THE CORTINA TROUBLE

G overnor Runnel's earlier victory over Sam Houston was not repeated, and the legendary Houston won the second race between them in August 1859. For the rest of the year Texas had a lame duck chief executive, and a number of things went wrong in a series of historical coincidences that ended Runnels' days in office on a bitter note. He had made a valiant effort to control the Indian problem with both hostile and friendly Indians, but dissatisfaction over Indian raids played a significant role in his loss to Houston. The federal government withdrew its army units from the Laredo/Brownsville region to take part in the expulsion of the agency Indians, leaving the river unprotected. Normally, this would have had no serious consequences, but this time it coincided with the emergence of a leader among the Mexican adventurers along the lower Rio Grande.

For a short while it seemed that the old dream of a Mexico reaching north to the Nueces might be a possibility. The force behind this vision was Juan Nepomuceno Cortina, known as "Cheno," who came from a fine family. His mother owned considerable property above Brownsville. She had married twice and had other sons besides Cheno. His half brothers were well-to-do members of the community, respected in Cameron County. Cheno never fitted into this family circle. In school he spent more time fighting than learning and was unable to read or write, but the good looking young man was popular. Giving up on education, he lived with mustangers and *rancheros* and became a leader among the lower classes along the Rio Grande.

During the Mexican War, Cortina had served as a corporal in the Mexican army and fought at Palo Alto and Resaca de la Palma. His activities during the rest of the war are unknown, and he next appears in 1848 after the war was over, working for the U.S. Army as a quartermaster employee bringing supplies and stores from Mexico. He was a good worker, quick to defend his rights and position. One army officer gave him high marks; another refused to pay him.

Following the war he became a minor player in the political affairs of the settlement that formed around Fort Brown, soon to be called Brownsville. In short order, two political factions emerged. Since few of the voters could read or write, the American party bosses used red and blue colors to distinguish the rival groups. At election time, much attention was paid to the Hispanic voters, who formed the majority of the population. Cheno could usually deliver fifty votes in an election and became a man of some importance. During this time, he worked with several Americans in a profitable horse and cattle enterprise, with scant regard for national boundaries. A falling out with some of his associates would soon have dire consequences.

He spent time at his mother's ranch while not engaged in his cattle "business." As it was not too distant, he often rode from the ranch to Brownsville for morning coffee. In mid July 1859, Cortina was in Brownsville and watched the town marshal arrest a former servant. The officer used an excessive amount of force and Cortina objected, at first politely. When the marshal answered in an offensive manner, the quick tempered Cortina shot him in the shoulder. Cortina ran for his horse, jerked the servant up behind him and galloped out of town.

It was a scene from a Western movie, a border ballad that made Cheno Cortina a hero on both sides of the Rio Grande. For almost two decades he would taunt ranger and soldier alike. He presented Governor Runnels with the final crisis of his term and brought the rangers back to the lower Valley.[1]

For the moment, however, Cortina was no problem and two months passed without further trouble. Cheno Cortina seemed to have vanished. Later it was learned he was raising troops to serve near Tampico, where he received money and supplies and had no trouble finding recruits. The already popular Cheno was now a folk hero, a man who shot a *gringo* marshal, but not everyone was enchanted with his sudden popularity. Miguel Tijerina, one of his cousins and commander of the Mexican cavalry in Matamoros, tried to get his kinsman to leave the border and go south, but Cheno delayed. It now seems evident he was planning an attack on Brownsville.

Early in the morning of September 28, Cortina and between seventy-five and one-hundred riders, depending on the source, rode into

Brownsville, Texas, about 1855, from a contemporary engraving.

Brownsville. A number of the townspeople were returning from a celebration across the river in Matamoros and ran into the riders coming down the road from Rio Grande City. The quiet was broken by screams, gunfire, the sound of breaking glass, and wild yells. People on the streets tried to find shelter as the horsemen galloped through the streets and alleys, shooting at anyone they saw, any lighted window, any hanging lamps. The attack took everyone by surprise and there was no resistance; the town fell under the control of the raiders.

The town marshal, the chief target, managed to escape as did Adolphus Glavaecke, Cortina's former business associate but now a deadly enemy. Three Americans were killed by Cortina or some of his followers. An Hispanic citizen tried to hide another American and was murdered for his effort. The outlaws broke into the jail, killed the jailer and liberated the prisoners. With no garrison, Fort Brown was easily taken. The Mexicans tried to enter the magazine but the walls and door were too massive.

Finally, Cortina's cousin, Colonel Miguel Tijerina, José María Jesús Carvajal, other military and civilian figures from Mexico as well as the Mexican consul in Brownsville talked Cortina into leaving Brownsville. He gathered his little army and rode out of the cowed and shot-up town. If he had been a folk hero before, the capture of

Brownsville made him a Mexican idol.

In an effort to prevent future attacks, the Brownsville citizens formed a town guard commanded by W.B. Thompson. They could muster only twenty men, but this small force was enough to keep Cortina outside town. A scout by the sheriff and some friendly *rancheros* and townsmen captured a man named Thomas Cabrera. The man was a lieutenant of Cortina, who threatened to burn the town if harm came to his associate. He remained outside the town, however, not wishing to fight the now confident "Brownsville Tigers."

Their confidence exceeded their abilities, although they did not learn this for a time. When Cheno failed to attack, the town guard decided to take the fight to him. They had some Mexican support; although Cortina was idolized by both the poor and the criminal elements, most of the landowners did not sympathize with him and even feared him. About forty-five Mexicans joined the "Tigers." A Mexican colonel came over from Matamoros bringing some men and a small field piece. The Americans managed to acquire another small cannon from the Fort Brown stores and started out to Cortina's camp up river, taking almost a week to go seven miles! When they neared what they thought was the enemy base the sheriff tried to lead them into battle, but when some shooting started, the mixed command fled towards Brownsville leaving behind the two cannon.[2]

The "fight" at Santa Rita was yet another jewel in the Cheno crown. In addition to his enhanced reputation, which now included a great victory in the open field, he had two cannon. Even before this abortive attempt to catch Cortina, Governor Runnels had decided something had to be done about the rapidly deteriorating situation in Cameron County. There was no way of knowing when U.S. Army units could return to the valley, and Runnels fell back on the only solution he had—the rangers.

The governor selected William G. Tobin to lead a company. In a plain statement of a new role—the rangers as peace officers— Runnels told the new captain he was to form a hundred man company and go to Cameron County and assist the civil authorities. Tobin was to quell disorder and arrest any of the lawless men responsible for the recent acts in the area. He was, however, "to be prudent and refrain from disturbing Mexican or American citizens or encroaching upon Mexican soil..." And, as always, the rangers would arm and equip themselves and look to the next legislature for payment.[3]

Tobin had been recommended as a ranger leader in 1855 and had commanded a small company for a month in October.[4] He was either the nearest ex-ranger to the scene, or Runnels had some other reason for selecting him for the mission. However chosen, Tobin began recruiting his company, formed officially on October 8, 1859, although Tobin had enlisted some men several days before. About half of the new rangers came from San Antonio. Samuel Jackson brought a considerable group from Seguin, and others came from various settlements. When company elections were held, Jackson was chosen 1st lieutenant.[5]

Formation of the new company and the march to Brownsville took some time, although news of the new company was common knowledge along the border. Its arrival could not happen soon enough for the people in Brownsville. Writing at night while sheltered in one of the town guardhouses, Mayor Stephen Powers wrote Runnels that the citizens hoped Tobin would soon reach them; a few citizens were on guard but could not handle the situation alone.

The mayor said the few Americans in town did not have enough weapons. Matters were so desperate they had asked the Mexican authorities in Matamoros for arms and had borrowed some old muskets and Mississippi Rifles, all in poor condition. The small stores of arms and ammunition in town had been exhausted. Powers mentioned the scout by the sheriff and the capture of Cabrera, who had played a prominent role in the raid on Brownsville and whose arrest had so enraged Cortina, now camped about nine miles above the town with several hundred followers. When Cortina threatened to burn the town, the Americans had swallowed their pride and asked for help from across the Rio Grande. The Mexicans sent sixty men, a field piece and a colonel to occupy Fort Brown.[6]

Powers' letter must have made sorry reading for Runnels, far distant in Austin, and the news did not get better. Tobin's company reached Brownsville without incident, but there was trouble following their arrival. Angered by Cortina's threats to burn the town, a mob took the jail and lynched Cabrera. Members of the mob were never officially identified or punished although there was some talk that a few of Tobin's men had been part of the gang.[7] Runnels' hope that the rangers would assist the local authorities was not to be real-

ized, and the incident was the beginning of a series that, rightly or
wrongly, would taint the rangers in Tobin's command. Some hint of
what would lie ahead is in a brief note in the Ranger Papers,
addressed to "Dr W."

> ...we are here in Brownsville and the town completely
> barricaded the people under arms...Poor Jackson is
> dead accidentally killed by being thrown from a car-
> riage yesterday in Matamoros, and the carriage run-
> ning over him producing intense hemmorage, so that
> we are now at a great—in regard to having a good
> officer. Tobin does well but has not the confidence of
> the men as Jackson had –

The writer asked his friend to come as quickly as possible, with all the
men he could. On a cheerful note, he concluded by noting the company was in general good health.[8]

A check of muster rolls reveals that the writer, "P. Jordan," was
Dr. Powhatan Jordan, Ford's surgeon, who had signed on again to
watch over the health of the rangers.[9] His reference to Jackson's
death is substantiated by other records showing the officer was acci-
dentally killed November 13, 1859. The same record lists Private John
Littleton as elected 1st lieutenant to replace Jackson the following
day.[10]

It is interesting to speculate what might have happened had not
Jackson been killed in an accident, a very un-ranger way to die! He
might have controlled the company better than did Tobin, even prevented some of the stain on the ranger name. Littleton took his place
and assumed the responsibilities of an officer, but his first independent command was not to be the stuff of legends.

On November 20, Tobin sent Lieutenant Littleton and thirty men
to escort Captain John Donaldson into Brownsville. Tobin had
received a report the officer was coming from Live Oak County with
thirty men and was a day away. The flat terrain, brush covered and cut
by numerous unmapped trails, was generally unfamiliar to the newly
arrived rangers, and Littleton and Donaldson marched on different
paths and never met. Donaldson, accompanied by Captain Henry
Berry and forty men from Nueces County, reached Brownsville with-

out incident. Still looking for Donaldson the following day, Littleton encountered what appeared to be a small party of Cortina's men. He had his men dismount, secure their horses, then charge the men in the chaparral. They discovered they were facing a considerable force, with artillery according to Littleton, and after a half hour of fighting at close quarters, the lieutenant ordered his men to fall back to their horses. Three men had been killed and were left on the field: William McKay, Thomas Grier and Nicholas R. Millet. John Fox was seriously wounded and either surrendered or was cut off and captured.

The next day, November 22, Tobin took his entire command and returned to the scene of the fight. He found the stripped and mutilated bodies of the dead rangers, whose horses, arms and equipment had been taken. The bodies were buried on the battlefield.[11]

The next few days saw considerable scouting, according to notations on the muster rolls, though little else remains to record the fighting. One of Tobin's men lost a horse in action on November 23.[12] Other ranger detachments were reaching the area, and a member of Captain Henry Berry's unit was wounded on the following day.[13] It is possible these two losses occurred when Tobin gathered a considerable force—his company and the Brownsville defenders with a howitzer from Fort Brown—and marched out to find Cortina. After an encounter, of sorts, at a place called Santa Rita, the Texans retreated in some disorder, according to Major Sam P. Heintzelman who would reach the Brownsville area in about two weeks and become the senior officer on the American side.[14]

Even though he had not been raiding, Cortina had not been idle and was at the pinnacle of his brief role as savior of the oppressed along the Rio Grande. It was a role he understood and played to the fullest, made easier because there was an element of truth in much of what he said. On November 23, 1859, Cortina issued a proclamation from Rancho del Carmen.[15] He reminded the Mexicans of their sufferings at the hands of oppressors and told them he had assumed the role of their protector. It was a surprisingly mild document, everything considered, and makes no suggestion he was trying to force the boundary north to the Nueces. Nothing suggests he wanted to drive away the Americans; instead, he hoped that Sam Houston would protect them when he became governor.

It is doubtful if anyone paid much attention to the proclamation

on either side of the Rio Grande, but Cortina continued to gain supporters and followers, not always the flower of society. A group of
prisoners broke out of a Mexican jail and joined up. Other Mexican
bands crossed the river, stayed until they had enough plunder to make
the trip profitable, then went home. The federal government sent
more troops to the region and put Major Sam P. Heintzelman in command. These forces reached the area on December 5, 1859.

Just what Tobin was doing in the days after returning to
Brownsville after the aborted scout to Santa Rita is unknown. In a
later report he mentioned his men were actively scouting. The scouts
had a dual purpose, to keep track of Cortina and to become familiar
with the country.[16] Berry's rangers were also active; a notation on his
muster roll shows five horses and a pack mule were killed on a forced
march in very cold weather on December 3, 1859.[17] Scant as they are,
these records indicate the rangers were doing something, even in
adverse weather.

No real action was taken against Cortina until December 14. It
took that long for the U.S. Army units to arrive on the scene and
make preparations. When the column finally moved out, it was a
mixed force containing parts of several ranger units, a company of
the 2nd Cavalry, infantry, dismounted artillery, one artillery detachment with howitzers, and the usual wagons and camp equipment. It
was a classic army force of the time, with only one cavalry company
suitable for the task of chasing mounted bandits. The command
marched at the pace of the slowest unit and was a long time on the
Laredo Road. Cortina had long since abandoned his camp when they
arrived.

In short order, however, they discovered the outlaw had not
moved far. Cortina, defended by his captured cannon, had selected a
strong position in the dense chaparral. When he opened fire, Major
Heintzelman dismounted the rangers and placed his own howitzers in
firing position. Cortina's cannon were silenced in the brief exchange
of fire. When the major ordered a charge, both the rangers and the
army soldiers rushed forward. Tobin reported the Texans were the
first to reach the now abandoned artillery position. The gunners had
managed to haul off the field pieces but had abandoned clothing and
other gear.

There were signs Cortina's men were regrouping up the trail, and

Heintzelman ordered the rangers to start in pursuit. The cavalry company, commanded by Captain George Stoneman, moved out on a parallel road. The rangers soon ran into a strong enemy position and came under heavy fire from the brush along the roadside. Hastily dismounting, Tobin sent his men through the thickets on foot. The fighting was intense, at close range, before the bandit rear guard broke and fled. The rangers had one man, Private David Herman, mortally wounded, another less severely wounded, and a horse killed.

In his report, Tobin states that shortly after this Major Heintzelman rode up and "ordered the men to halt for dinner!" It was the end of the fight. Tobin commended his men for their part in the affair and specifically mentioned Captain Peter Tumlinson for his role in the fighting.[18] Tobin closed his report to Runnels by describing how difficult it was to operate in the chaparral country. While the fighting was taking place, reinforcements were close at hand but unable to force their way through the brush until after Cortina had escaped. The mention of reinforcements close by accounts for Tobin's rather puzzling notation that Ford had arrived and assumed command of state troops.

Tobin's report has played little or no part in the accounts of the Cortina troubles, and it is in complete disagreement with later U.S. Army versions which cast Tobin's rangers as incompetent cowards. In Major Heintzelman's reconstructed final account, the rangers had been so "stampeded" by their previous expedition it was only with the greatest difficulty he managed to get them to move! He explained the enemy resistance was quite light, and that the rangers finally managed to move after being encouraged by the coolness of the army regulars.[19] He evidently did not know Tobin had written the ranger side of the fight. Tobin's report has generally been disregarded and has never been published, and Heintzelman's self serving account has become history.

The Texas Legislature was in session during November 1859, and many people were in Austin for the occasion. Ford was busy greeting friends and discussing the latest rumors about Cortina. The many tales and often exaggerated reports had caused several ranger units to be formed earlier in the month, but the most recent horror story had the outlaws taking and burning Corpus Christi! Ford managed to convince Forbes Britton, a resident of Corpus, that his family was safe, but just then Governor Runnels walked by and Forbes rushed over and began an impassioned speech about his family's being burned out!

Runnels listened for a moment and turned to the ranger.

"Ford, you must go; you must start tonight, and move swiftly."

The ranger assured the governor he would leave as soon as he could obtain a horse.

This part of the action was highly informal, as Ford remembered it, but Runnels quickly put matters in regular channels to bring Ford back into service and raise additional ranger units. He authorized Ford to form a standard company of seventy-four privates with the necessary complement of officers, sergeants, corporals, buglers and farriers. A duplicate authorization was sent to S.B. Highsmith.[21]

Runnels attached instructions regarding the ranger units already in service in the valley. The main provisions were:

> Units formed in Bexar, Victoria, Gonzales and other counties would be admitted into the service.
>
> As nearly as possible, Ford would reorganize these commands on the U.S. Army model.
>
> Upon reorganization, the men would elect their officers and their field officers.
>
> When the force was organized, the commanding officer would appoint quartermaster, paymaster, etc.
>
> Until the force was organized and officers elected, Ford was authorized to contract for necessary supplies.
>
> Ford was to rank as major until the above services had been completed and the organization completed.

The newly appointed Major Ford started south the day after he was authorized to assume command of the state troops. The assignment was somewhat similar to his earlier experience when he had left with an ill-armed handful; this time Ford had eight volunteers armed with a few rifles and some pistols. On the way to Goliad he picked up a few recruits, and by the time he arrived in Banquete, twenty-four miles west of Corpus Christi, his command numbered fifty-three men all armed and riding serviceable horses. They obtained some needed supplies and learned Highsmith would not be raising a company.

The company was formally organized and mustered into service at Banquete on November 30, 1859. Joseph Walker was chosen captain. Ford, commanding all the state troops, was not a candidate.[22] They broke camp around December 1, as near as Ford could recall in later years, and started for Brownsville, but he may have remembered the actual date incorrectly. The following day they resumed the march and heard cannon firing after an hour on the trail; there were signs spies were trailing them, and every precaution was taken to prevent surprise. They were not familiar with the country and were hesitant about striking out through the chaparral. When they neared Brownsville, they galloped into town and created a panic among the men of the town company hastily formed to halt what they believed was another Cortina raid. Cheering broke out when it was learned the attackers were ranger reinforcements. In town, Ford learned the firing they had heard was from Major Heintzelman's army troops who had gone looking for Cortina. He led his men at a fast pace and reached the battle ground just after the fight was over.[23]

Back in town, Ford reported on his actions after leaving Austin. He announced the arrival of the company under Walker and their actions to reach the battlefield. The major reported he had assumed command of all state troops and was cooperating with Major Henintzelman. Heavy rains had turned the already poor roads into bogs which, combined with the advance of the artillery and "the unprepared condition of part of the command," induced Major Heintzelman "to suggest returning to this place, which I conceived entirely proper." He added that Tobin would no doubt make a report of his operations.[24]

Both Tobin and Ford stated the other would probably file reports of their operations. Ford evidently took Heintzelman's unsubstantiated statement of the "unprepared part of the command" at face value and did not check with either Tobin or Tumlinson to find out the true condition of the other two ranger units.

Ford and the army major agreed on plans to combat Cortina, much the same arrangement Heintzelman had previously with Tobin. By general agreement, the army officer was recognized as the senior commander in the region and began writing orders and correspondence in the name of "Headquarters Brownsville Expedition." Order No. 4 directed Ford, Tobin and Captain Stoneman to make sweeps towards Point Isabel and the areas containing the shipping and customs offices. It was feared Cortina might slip down and capture considerable currency stores in the customs house, but after several days of intensive scouting, it was clear the outlaw chief was not in the area.[25]

When definite word of Cortina's location came in, Heintzelman began making efforts to follow him up river. On December 20, 1859, Ford signed a contract for thirty Sharps carbines and considerable quantities of caps and prepared cartridges.[26] According to his *Memoirs*, they started up the river the same day.

Major Heintzelman took all the rangers and troops he had in the area. The companies commanded by Tobin and Tumlinson rode on the road between Brownsville and Rio Grande City. Ford commanded the right flank with Walker's company and a Victoria unit led by G.J. Hampton. After a time out in the brush, literally forcing their way through dense thickets, it became clear their guide was deliberately wandering about. Ford told the man to either get them back on the main road or he was going to let his men follow their instincts and shoot him!

Besides the ranger units mentioned by Ford in the early stages of the march, other units or detachments were in the combined force. Andrew Herron, commanding a unit formed at Ringgold Barracks, and William R. Henry, of Callahan's expedition, were also in the action. On the third day of the march, the column began to see evidence of widespread looting and vandalism. Houses and fences had been burned, property destroyed or carried off. The countryside was deserted; the raiders were making no racial distinctions and were killing both Hispanics and Americans. The column halted the evening of December 26 about eighteen miles below Rio Grande City. Cortina had a strong defensive position in and around the town.

That evening, Heintzelman held a council of war, deciding to send three companies to circle Cortina's position in the town in order to maneuver behind him and block the road from Rio Grande City to Roma. These were the ranger companies of Joe Walker, Hampton and Herron, to be commanded by Ford.[27] Ford said he had about ninety men in the three units; apparently many of the men in the three companies were absent on other duties.

With Ford were H. Clay Davis, a veteran who knew the area and James McClusky, the sutler from Ringgold Barracks. They would be of great help in guiding the rangers. Davis led them off the road, where they visited a ranch owned by a friendly Mexican. The rancher told them he had just returned from Rio Grande City and explained the disposition of Cortina's forces. The outlaw had his main body in town, with his left flank anchored on a hill north of town and his right on the Rio Grande. Because of the dense chaparral, it seemed impossible to circle through the brush and attack his rear, as planned. The open ground before the settlement was defended by a strong picket, as was the road entering Rio Grande City. Ford was afraid any turning movement through the brush would alert Cortina and give him time to run. He was determined to force a fight.

Ford moved his rangers through the brush to within a few hundred yards of the advanced picket defending the road. The Texans literally slept on their feet, holding their bridles, quieting their horses and nodding until just before daylight. Back along the road they heard the rumble of the regular army's artillery guns, caissons and supply wagons. Ford rode back and explained the disposition of Cortina's forces to Heintzelman and decided to return to the original plan for a sweep of the left flank of the enemy. The major agreed and placed Ford in command of all the ranger units.

Led by an advance guard, the Texans moved along the road and dispersed the picket blocking the way into town. Hearing the firing, Cortina sent out a strong reconnaissance party which was engaged at Ringgold Barracks on the outskirts of town. A brief firefight scattered this group, sending them back through the streets. Now at the edge of the settlement, the rangers came under random sniper fire from rooftops. Moving rapidly, some of the rangers reached the top of a small hill and could see the town had been abandoned. Questioning several inhabitants, the rangers received only shrugs until one of the Americans in town approached to tell them Cortina had retreated to some large ebony trees outside the town.

Once again, Cortina had selected a strong defensive position. His right flank was secured by the river, his left was in a cemetery. His center, generally across the road going to Roma, was held by infantry and his two cannon. It was still early in the morning and much of the area was covered with fog. Ford sent Tobin to circle and attack the left flank, while he moved along the road to penetrate the main position. The rangers moved quickly through the fog and the brush, trying to see. They were within two-hundred yards of the enemy cannon before they knew the exact location of the enemy's line, revealed by cannon fire through the fog. Ford was in the advance, about thirty yards from one gun, and was hit in several places by buckshot. Fortunately for the Texans, the guns had been poorly loaded, and much of the iron and buckshot went high.

Ford had brought much of his command into the frontal attack, but the placement of the cannon changed his plan. He knew enough not to charge cannon with horsemen and diverted his mounted rangers to his right, out of the line of fire. He sent a detachment of dismounted rangers to take shelter behind a fence line and engage the outlaws with their rifles. These Texans were mostly armed with Minie Rifles, an infantryman's weapon, fairly quick to load and deadly accurate; with their rifles the rangers began cutting up the cannon crews and the supporting infantry. Ford then had most of the mounted rangers dismount and charge the left flank of the artillery position. The fog was still heavy, and powder smoke from the cannon and small arms dropped visibility to a few yards, particularly around the guns. In this close fighting, a number of the rangers were hit by buckshot or metal fragments.

The rifle fire and the sudden rush from the flank either killed or scared off the gun crews and those around them. Cortina must have been closely monitoring the action because he sent a mounted force towards the rangers, but Ford had been around Mexican army forces for years and recognized the bugle calls that were blaring through the fog and smoke. He began gathering his men and pulling back into the chaparral. The rangers forced their mounts into the dense brush and took position just inside the thicket. They were receiving some fire from all sides by now, and Ford told his men they could whip the enemy in that shape as in any other, and they turned back to wait the cavalry charge.

The Mexican horsemen came at a gallop, right at the dimly seen rangers. The Texans waited and then used their revolvers at close range, shattering the massed formation. In a moment, riderless horses were crashing into the brush, turning back into the still advancing cavalrymen and smashing into other mounts beside them. The charge slowed just as Tobin came up behind the rangers with some of his men. It had been a slow struggle through the brush, but they reached the field in time to blunt what was left of the outlaw charge. Peter Tumlinson was on foot, using a rifle. The rest of Tobin's unit soon rushed up, and the horsemen, those still able, broke and fled.

The cavalry charge and the temporary withdrawal of the rangers into the brush left the two cannon unprotected. Some of the Mexicans managed to rush the prized guns from the field, even though most of the force was attempting to escape. Many of the rangers started after them on foot, but Ford called them back and began reforming and remounting his men. Major Heintzelman rode up, and Ford reported what had happened. Strangely enough, the major said he had not heard any firing! He did approve the ranger's plan to pursue the fleeing outlaws.

During his talk with Heintzelman, Ford noticed some Mexican footmen just emerging from the water on the Mexican side and others running down the banks on the Texas side. He suggested to Captain Stoneman, who had ridden up, that something should be done. In the army's only contribution to the fight, Stoneman had his soldiers open fire with their Sharps and killed some of the fleeing men.

As soon as they could find their horses and regroup into some kind of formation, the rangers started out on the Roma road, trying to cut off stragglers and catch the artillery crews and the two guns. Cortina made every effort to save his cannon. Several miles out from Rio Grande City, where the road crossed a ravine creating a natural defense position, Cortina made a stand, placing the guns to cover the road and rallying running men to serve as a guard. By now, all the ranger units had reformed and were in the chase. Lieutenant Littleton was in the lead and had his rifle hit by an enemy shot. Captain Henry was another officer well to the front. Despite heavy fire, the rangers charged up the road, crossed the ravine and scattered Cortina's personal body guard and the unorganized group about the cannon. One gun was captured in place, but the desperate crew of the other weapon managed to start their gun down the road. Henry rode up, dismounted, and had the captured gun turned about and fired at the retreating outlaws. The shot caused them to run, abandoning the other cannon.

There were still stragglers all along the road and in the brush. The road to Roma was not secure, and Ford was afraid the bandits might rob the little settlement. He gathered a strong party and moved as rapidly as possible up the road, arriving before any large number of Cortina's band could enter. It was a wise precaution, but unnecessary. Cortina had fled into the brush, away from the river. Those of his followers still alive crossed the Rio Grande as best they could. The outlaw commander had lost his two cannon, his personal papers, small arms, supplies, horses and an unknown number of men.[28]

Most damaging of all, he lost his shield of invincibility. The earlier fight at the log barricade could be explained away since he had brought off his cannon and the Americans had not pursued. This time, however, he had lost everything, and his men were scattered and running for their lives. His casualties were never known but were extremely heavy. It was not a one sided fight; the rangers had sixteen men wounded, several severely. Ford and his adjutant were hurt, as was Henry. Three men in Tobin's company were hit; Tumlinson had one wounded. Walker had four shot, as did Herron, and Henry had one man slightly injured.[29]

As revealed by the lists of the injured, it was the rangers who had fought the battle, with most or all of the companies in the fighting. In an after action report, Major Heintzelman was lavish in his praise of Ford and the Texans, saying they swept everything before them, capturing the enemy guns, wagons and baggage.[30] Some two months later, however, he had a considerably different version which downplayed the Texan's part in defeating Cortina.[31]

On January 1, 1860, Heintzelman wrote Ford informing him he had received recent news of Cortina and his followers. According to Mexican sources, Cheno had about thirty followers with him, the rest of his large band had been scattered. The major suggested that sending out many small patrols was the best way to intercept and keep dispersed the remnants of the outlaw force. He was especially interested in capturing Cortina. Heintzelman informed Ford of recent changes in the location of U.S. Army troops.[32]

During this period, Ford was the acknowledged commander of the state troops. However, in Runnel's instructions sending Ford to the valley, an election for major was specified once all the units had been assembled or as soon as possible. Evidently a new order to hold an election was sent down from Austin. This letter is referenced in correspondence of the time, though the instructions seem to have been lost. Ford merely said, "the efficiency of the Texas rangers was materially lessened by the order for an election for major."[33] Tobin refers to "instructions from the Governor," in a later letter.

With the rangers assembled in Rio Grande City, Ford started writing his report of the recent battle. During this time, there was much campaigning for votes in the upcoming election for major. Tobin was the chief candidate. For whatever reasons, Ford did not make any effort to campaign, or that was the way he remembered it much later. Lieutenant Littleton was eager to become a captain, which could only occur if Tobin was elected the major and vacated his old position for a new man. Peter Tumlinson was another likely choice but did not seem interested. Ford said he suggested that both he and Tobin resign and run for office, with the loser's entering the ranks as a private. Tobin declined.[34]

From his rather detailed explanations about his views on discipline, it seems likely Ford lost votes among the less orderly rangers,[35] and when the election was over Tobin had won by six votes. He immediately assumed command and dispatched Tumlinson's company on a scout. He sent a message to Major Heintzelman, informing him of his new rank and position and offering to cooperate with the army.[36] The army officer answered the same day from Roma, making the same suggestion about small patrols he had earlier given Ford.[37]

The day after the election, Ford gathered most of the rangers in the hayloft in the army barracks in Rio Grande City and read them a copy of his report on the fighting outside the town and the defeat of Cortina. Ford said he mentioned everyone who had performed properly, without casting aspersions on anyone, enlisted or officer. The account left several of the rangers wondering why Ford had not read the report earlier, saying it would have won him the election.[38]

The victory at Rio Grande City and the election of Tobin resulted in the break up of the ranger forces. Several interpretations can be placed on what happened. It is possible that Ford was a poor loser and refused to serve under Tobin and started back to Brownsville, followed by most of Walker's company. He did mention that since Tobin had declined to accept his offer of resigning and serving as a private if losing the election, he therefore did not feel compelled to remain in service. Walker's men also claimed they had not been enlisted for a specific term and could leave when they wished. Besides, they believed Cortina was finished.[39]

Ford may also have believed that more action was ahead, and he wanted to be near the scene. Whatever his motives he went downstream with a considerable number of armed men who were no longer officially Texas Rangers. There was no way they could have known that Sam Houston, now governor, was examining the entire situation in the valley and considering a drastic shuffling of the ranger forces.

The same day Tobin sent his letter to Heintzelman announcing his assumption of command, Houston appointed two commissioners to go to the valley and examine everything pertaining to the fight against Cortina. They had extensive powers to muster in state troops or to discharge any units in service. Angel Navarro and Robert H. Taylor left for Brownsville as fact finders and judges.[40]

It was a good day for official communications. Tobin must have known Houston was now governor because he reported his election as major on January 2, 1860, and stated Ford had been his opponent. Tobin also complained that Ford had not held an election immediately on arriving in the valley. "What his object could be in disregarding those instructions I leave to those acquainted with the matter to determine." He reported he had mustered out the units commanded by Hampton and Herron, as well as Walker's company. Tobin included a lengthy section on the difficulties of campaigning along the Rio Grande. He concluded by hoping the government would protect the citizens and compel the Mexican government to take action as well.[41]

In an age of slow communication, Houston was trying to control a distant situation where events outran couriers. On December 30, 1859, believing Ford was still commanding all the rangers, he wrote Ford that Captain Alexander C. Hill was bringing a proclamation in English and Spanish that he hoped would help end the troubles.[42] Captain Hill was also now the leader of a spy company and Houston, convinced of his ability, allowed him to contract for supplies and rations for twenty-one men and horses.[43]

The new governor's proclamation promised all who had taken part in the recent disturbances that no immediate action would be taken against them if they went home in peace. The same day he authorized the formation of a new ranger company for duty on the northern frontier.[44]

When now Captain Hill reached Brownsville, he found a completely new situation. Ford had already discovered how conditions had changed when he and the others reached the town. Navarro and Taylor were already on the scene to greet them, along with many of the local citizens. Ford remembered the reception as cordial. Unlike many in the area, he did not believe Cortina was finished. To the contrary, as they rode down from Rio Grande City, there was evidence the outlaw leader was regrouping and recruiting.

For a time, there was a strange situation. Walker had enough of ranger service and headed north for Austin, accompanied by some of his company. Most of the remaining men of the unofficial band camped outside of Brownsville, waiting to see what would develop. Ford retained control of the state's supplies, equipment and arms, as well as public animals.[45]

Meanwhile, the two commissioners had been busy. They had reached Brownsville in the short time of seven days and were first met with threats rather than courtesy. Most people believed they had come to negotiate with Cortina. Taylor reported all this to Houston, outlining what they found and their recommendations for future action.[46] The commissioners formed an opinion, after talking with numerous people, that there was no command supervision of the rangers and that some of the Texans were causing as much damage as Cortina's men. There were still three companies left, or so they thought, and nothing was being done. Accordingly, they had ordered Major Tobin and the other ranger units to report to Brownsville to be mustered out.

Taylor described the devastated condition of the lower Rio Grande region up to Rio Grande City. No crops could be made, and all the cattle and horses had been driven across into Mexico. The Americans had been killed or driven away, and the few "Mexicans" still in the area lived in daily fear of their lives. The commissioners were satisfied the Mexican authorities knew every move of Cortina and allowed him to be supplied with arms and ammunition from stores in Matamoros. In an effort to establish some semblance of order, the commissioners were forming two new ranger companies. In a postscript to his letter Taylor asked the governor to make some effort to pay the troops, "as the citizens skin them every chance they get at them." Taylor reported what had happened as well as what was planned. Four days earlier he and Navarro had written Tobin a brief note ordering him to report with his command and be mustered out in Brownsville.[47]

The decision to form two companies to patrol the river was based on the unsettled condition in the area. A few days after their first report they wrote Houston again, describing how the mail carrier was stopped only twenty-four miles from Brownsville. They estimated Cortina now had about 150 armed men and seemed preparing for a fight. They reported they would probably be detained longer than anticipated because of this news.[48]

On January 20, 1860, the commissioners began swearing in men for a new ranger company. The cadre for the unit was about thirty privates from Walker's old command, and enough others enlisted to bring the first day's strength to fifty. On February 1, a contingent arrived from Corpus Christi. The company eventually had eighty-two privates plus the authorized officers, sergeants and corporals, a sergeant major and a hospital steward.[49] Old Rip was the captain.

As usual, there was no public money and Ford had some difficulty finding mules. The local merchants were extremely grateful for ranger protection, but they did not let patriotism stand before profit. Ford needed pack animals and told his quartermaster to pay whatever was required. Some mules were purchased for a hundred dollars, which Ford considered extortion.[50]

A second ranger company was formed on February 1, 1860. John Littleton, elected to command Tobin's old company after the election for major, had brought his men down river after Ford and sat about in the Brownsville area until the commissioners disbanded all the rangers and then selected him to lead the second of the new companies. His unit was to be part of Ford's new command.[51] On February 2, the commissioners wrote Ford that from that date his troops and those under his command would be directed by Major Heintzelman, or the commanding officer of the U.S. troops on the border.[52] Ford took this to mean he was commanding all the state troops in the region.

While the reorganization was taking place, Cortina had been busy with his own regrouping. It was common knowledge he had at least the unofficial support of Mexican authorities, as reported by Commissioner Taylor. The location of some of his forces along the Rio Grande became of concern to American authorities. At the time, steamboats regularly traveled up the Rio Grande to Rio Grande City. The King and Kennedy Line had a steamer, the *Ranchero*, anchored at Rio Grande City until it was safe to move down to Brownsville with $300,000 in coin aboard plus valuable freight and a number of passengers. The river flowed in a series of great curves, with some banks high enough to overlook the deck of a steamer. One of these twists was large enough to be named—the Bolsa Bend—and was the spot where the outlaws seemed most likely to attack the steamer as it moved towards Brownsville.

A mixed force of rangers and U.S. Army cavalry left for the Bend around February 1.[53] Captain George Stoneman and his company had been joined by Captain Manning M. Kimmel, also from the 2nd Cavalry. Ford had the men who had stayed on from Walker's company, around thirty rangers, and Littleton was along with a few men from his company. Hill's spy company was in the vicinity and was expected to join the column as soon as possible. The army cavalry moved along the road, with the pack animals and wagons, while Ford led the rangers along the river bank searching for any raiders. Along the way, Ford and some others visited Cortina's mother at her ranch. It was his opinion, as well as that of most knowledgeable people in the valley, that she had no part in her son's activities.

The rangers encountered and scattered several small bandit groups as they moved up the Rio Grande, killing a number of men on the march. About one o'clock in the afternoon of February 4, Ford ordered his pack animals to halt near a ranch close to Bolsa Bend, the location where he expected an attack on the *Ranchero* now steaming slowly downstream. Corporal Milam Duty, age twenty, was in charge of the rangers' pack animals and some wagons. As he approached the ranch buildings, Duty saw some thirty outlaws fording the Rio Grande, moving a herd of stolen horses into Mexico. He immediately charged them and opened fire, driving them away from the animals still on the Texas shore. There was some return fire but no ranger casualties.

At this time, the men leading Tobin and Tumlinson's companies, on their way to Brownsville to be mustered from service, came in sight. Tobin rode over and conferred with Duty to learn what had happened. While they were talking, firing began again along the bank where Tobin's men had started shooting at the Mexicans on the opposite shore. A general firefight developed, with both sides shooting at anything they could see. In this exchange Ranger Fountain B. Woodruff was mortally wounded.[54]

The *Ranchero* came in sight during the fighting, an easy target for enemy riflemen along the high banks on the Mexican side of the river. As soon as the vessel was in the bend, she was fired upon. Unknown to anyone, the vessel was carrying the two field pieces captured from Cortina which he had earlier captured from the Texans. An army artillery detail was on board, commanded by Lieutenant Louis L. Langdon who may have anticipated some such situation because his guns were in action in short order and temporarily silenced the Mexican fire.

Despite the lull in the firing, everyone on board knew the real danger was just ahead as the steamer worked her way through the huge bend in the river where the banks were no more than 150 yards apart. The river bank on the Mexican side was overgrown in brush, with numerous houses, farm buildings and fences along the higher ground. Tall trees provided additional concealment for snipers. A courier had been sent to alert Ford to the situation, and he rode up around three in the afternoon.

Lieutenant Langdon went ashore and asked the ranger if he intended to cross into Mexico. Ford told him certainly; it was the only way attackers could be kept down or driven away. Ford knew this, just as he knew he did not have enough men with only parts of two ranger companies, and with Hill's spy company not expected until evening. Captain Stoneman's company was on a scout and would not be back until the following day. While there were parts of Tobin's and Tumlinson's command present, most of the men knew they were being discharged and declined to cross into Mexico. However, both captains volunteered to help and crossed the river with a few hardy souls to scout the opposite shore. Ford followed as quickly as he could gather his men, bringing about thirty-five rangers.

Advancing towards what he thought was Cortina's position, Ford ran into Tobin who told him the enemy had gone. It soon became clear to Ford that Cortina had merely shifted position because he could see a number of Mexican outlaws behind a fence and near some buildings. The rangers were moving in a single file when Ford had them do a right face and advance in a line at right angles to their previous advance. The ranger had discovered Cortina's right, protected by fifty to sixty horsemen, and shifted direction to strike the vulnerable flank. For some reason, the Mexican cavalry remained in position until the rangers had completed their maneuver.

The rangers were at right angles to the Mexican line, sheltered by the river bank, and could fire kneeling with little exposure, dropping down to reload. Most of the rangers had Sharps breech loaders, easy to recharge. Ford cautioned them to take their time, aim carefully, and make each round count. The Mexicans had now discovered the Texans and were firing wildly, loading and shooting as rapidly as possible, causing some concern on the steamer where some believed the Texans were being massacred. At one point, someone on the *Ranchero* began screaming for cartridges and led a few rangers to think they were short on ammunition. Ford stopped this budding panic in short order.

Ford had Littleton on the ranger right with orders to slowly turn the enemy left flank. About a dozen riflemen were detailed to keep the enemy horsemen under fire. Tobin and Tumlinson took an active part, fighting as individuals. The older Tumlinson chided Ford for entering the fight without a weapon! At some points the lines were no more than thirty yards apart, but the rangers had the advantage of a sheltered position, better weapons and calm direction. Despite the disparity in numbers, they began to cut into the Cortina forces. Ford had sent a message to the steamer captain to steam up and allow the artillerymen to use the cannon, but before this could be done the Mexicans began scattering.

Some of the Americans arrived at the river bank and opened fire across the water on Cortina's left flank. The enemy began to lose heart, and when their horsemen fled in disorder Ford decided it was time for a decisive charge. The rangers advanced at a run, firing their revolvers. They could see the people behind the fence start to give way. Ford, Littleton and Lieutenant Howard climbed the second bank and came under heavy fire, fortunately high. Ford had the others drop down until the Mexicans had emptied their muzzle loaders, then they charged, yelling and again using their six-shooters at close range. The Cortina forces, those still fighting, broke and scattered in the brush and growing darkness. The rangers followed as long as they could see, determined no one would be able to reform.

Juan "Cheno" Cortina has been called many things, but no man ever said he lacked courage. Riding a fine horse and screaming to his fleeing men, Cortina tried to get even a few to stay and fight until he was the last man, turning and firing at the rangers until his revolver was empty. It was almost night, with limited visibility, and the growing darkness may have saved him. The rangers continued to fire at him as he finally galloped into the night. Five rounds hit the outlaw or his horse, none serious, and he would live to fight another day . . . and another.

Ford was busy for a time. He exchanged notes with John Martin, captain of the *Ranchero*, who had requested help for his trip down the river. Ford offered his assistance and asked Martin to use the steamer to transport his men to the Mexican side.[55] He found time to dispatch a brief report to Heintzelman, describing the fight, the wounding of one ranger, and his belief the steamer required an escort down the Mexican bank to arrive safely in Brownsville. He suggested troops come up and march down the American side as well.[56] The ranger commander met with the two army officers present, who agreed to Ford's plan. The cavalrymen were to go down river on the American side, taking the wagons and pack mules. Stoneman promised Ford he would come to his aid if the outlaws attacked him. When Heintzelman received the report, he approved Ford's proposed plan but cautioned Ford to stay near the river, to keep his men under rigid control, and to avoid damage to property or people.[57] The following day, February 5, the major sent another note telling Ford he had talked with the senior Mexican commander, who assured him troops had been dispatched to restore order. Accordingly, he ordered the rangers to return to Texas.[58]

In the confusion, Ford may not have received this message in time to act, because during the night of February 4/5 he sent a patrol across the river but found nothing threatening. Feeling more secure, the rangers crossed back with their horses on February 5, prepared to escort the *Ranchero* downriver.

With the steamer between them, the soldiers and the Texans marched along the Rio Grande. The rangers were very cautious, fearing an ambush, and Ford and his forty-eight men did not make good time. A little distance below the great bend, they came on Las Palmas, a large ranch, and created a commotion among the ranch people, who started running from one of the main buildings. Ford wrote a note, which was translated into Spanish, telling the people he had not come to fight them, only Cortina. As some calm was being restored, a norther blew in and drove the steamer onto a sand bar opposite the ranch.

Trying to decide what to do following this unexpected act of nature, the rangers and the soldiers were halted around ten in the morning.[59] An official from Matamoros rode up. He could have been one of those dispatched by the Mexican commander, though Ford had no way of knowing about this development. The man, who identified himself as a police official, asked time to talk with his superiors and obtain permission for the rangers to stay in Mexico. It was clear the steamer could not be floated free that day, and both sides agreed to wait.

About six-hundred armed men were in plain view of the rangers, and the Mexican policeman identified them as Mexican soldiers. Ford asked about another two hundred to the rear of the rangers, but the official became very vague. It was clear to the Texans the men were Cortina followers, and the situation began to take a turn for the worse. Hill with his spy company, which had joined Ford at Las Palmas and formed a picket guard, reported that some Mexican irregulars threatened the Texans; Rip wanted to know why he had not opened fire!

Despite the potential for another pitched battle, the night ended without further incident. On the next day, February 6, Mexican officials met with Ford and Stoneman. With the army officer's full approval, even suggestion, the ranger did the talking and explained why he had crossed into Mexico. None too tactfully he mentioned it was common knowledge Mexican authorities did nothing to stop Cortina's raiding, and if this continued a war would break out between the two countries. In the end, the Mexicans gave the rangers permission to march down the river, on both banks if desired, but they also promised to protect the steamer if the Texans returned to the American side. Ford accepted this offer.

By the time all the talking was over, the *Ranchero* had been freed from the sand bar and was waiting to resume the voyage. The vessel and her escort reached Brownsville on February 8.[60]

Captain Hill reported to Houston the next day, probably the first free time he had enjoyed since reaching the valley. The captain told the governor his proclamation had been well received and had given new hope to people in the lower valley.[61] He informed the governor that Cortina had offered to make a treaty with Houston—if he was paid $4,000 and the men who had insulted him were punished! Hill said the outlaw was still raiding but was not the only one; others were active and blaming Cortina for their work. He assured the governor their crossing into Mexico had been justified by officials on both sides of the Rio Grande. Hill listed his expenses and included a list of the men currently in his detachment. There were twenty names, nine of them Spanish surnames. Muster rolls indicate his detachment was disbanded on February 1, an earlier date which may have been an effort to obtain pay for his men.[62] They do not figure in subsequent incidents concerning Cortina.

The other ranger units had little time to rest in Brownsville. The same day they arrived, Major Heintzelman issued an order sending the two units up to Edinburg, Ford's company above the town and Littleton's fifteen miles south. The ranger commanders could move as necessary to graze their horses and cover the area, but they were cautioned to stay on the Texas shore.[63]

The following day, Heintzelman sent a sharp note to one of the senior Mexican commander in Matamoros, absolving Ford of any blame for the burning of fences and some buildings in the fight at Bolsa Bend. The major reprimanded the official for the obvious complicity of Mexican authorities in Cortina's activities.[64]

Upriver, the two ranger companies continued patrolling, and Ford continued to drill his men as usual. Late in the month, Houston wrote and asked some pointed questions about service along the Rio Grande.[65] The governor wanted to know if Heintzelman regarded the rangers as being in federal government service. He wanted to know if Ford had ever acted under written orders; if so, copies were to be forwarded to Austin. Ford was to be asked by letter if Texas troops were necessary on the border. Houston said Ford would perceive the objective of these inquiries. At this time, it seems Houston could have been laying the foundation for another request for the U.S. Army to pay the rangers, If the Texans were not needed, Houston wanted them off the state's payroll; he was having troubles enough trying to support other ranger units along the northern frontier.

Houston was also concerned about earlier problems with the rangers in south Texas. On March 5, 1860, he wrote Tobin asking specific questions about the hanging of Cabrera and other Mexicans, his relationship with Heintzelman, the discipline of his troops, and details of the battle at Rio Grande City.[66] There is nothing in the archives to show Tobin replied or even received the letter. Nor is there anything to show Ford answered Houston's letter to him.

While waiting to see what Cortina would do, Ford kept his men busy scouting and practicing drills and maneuvers. During a simulated charge, his horse stepped in a hole and threw him. Ford was in a sorry state for weeks and had not fully recovered when spies brought word Cortina was at a small ranch called La Mesa, only four miles south of the ranger camp. About the same time, Ford received the same information through official Mexican sources. He was suspicious of this intelligence, however, fearing it was a trap.

The day following the message, Stoneman and Kimmel arrived, surprised to find the rangers still in camp. Ford explained he was awaiting orders to cross the Rio Grande, and Stoneman told him the orders had arrived. Still in some pain, the ranger allowed the cavalryman to handle the river crossing. The army's soldiers cut through the high bank, making a passage just wide enough for a single horse to slide down to the water. All of this took time, and it was three in the morning before the two ranger companies and the two army units were across into Mexico.

Ford's men led the march, with an advance party under Dan Givens.[67] The ranger spoke Spanish and was considered fearless and self possessed.[68] Givens scouted the area and returned to report there was a Mexican detachment ahead. When Stoneman came up, Ford suggested they avoid the ambush to their front. They circled and followed a path along the river, planning to enter La Mesa from the opposite side. While on this new course, they saw lights off to one side. Lieutenant Matthew Nolan was sent to investigate, and the enemy picket broke and ran. As the rangers started chasing the fleeing men, they heard drums beating an alarm in the ranch grounds.

Forming in line, the rangers advanced towards the buildings. There were no challenges by either side, and firing began when they were close enough to make out forms. The Mexicans knew the men coming in from the brush were Americans and started shooting. In a steady advance, the rangers routed the men outside the scattered buildings. A formed infantry force resisted for about ten minutes, then fled. Horsemen held the right flank for a time, then they ran. Men began throwing down weapons and equipment. Some ran for the shelter of buildings, men and women mixed in a wild rush. There were a few who still resisted, and in the last exchanges of fire one woman was killed.

Some of the rangers, searching the buildings, hauled a protesting Mexican officer from beneath a bed. The man demanded to see Colonel Ford and told the ranger captain he was a major, had been asleep, and the Texans were lucky he had not been awake or they would have been whipped! When he finished this tirade, he complained the Texans had taken his sword and robbed him.

When the army soldiers rode up, Ford told Stoneman they had "played old Scratch," killed a mule, wounded a woman, and had a fight with the Mexican *Guardia Nacional.* It was somewhat more than a fight—they had killed a number of the guardsmen, captured and wounded others. Nolan had shot the mule, but he justified this act by claiming it was night and he thought he was shooting a Mexican.

In the still early hours of morning, the rangers and army cavalrymen were making coffee when Stoneman's troopers began to mount hastily and prepare for a fight. Scouts had been watching for the Mexican force Givens had located during the night and had seen five or six-hundred mounted men advancing towards the ranch. A horseman rode ahead of the column, and the rangers waved him through their sentries. The Mexican introduced himself as the adjutant of the colonel commanding the horsemen. He said his superior wanted to talk with Colonel Ford. The ranger diplomatically informed him Stoneman was the senior American officer. The adjutant told them his superior held Ford responsible for what had happened and would speak only with him.

Stoneman seemed only too happy with this arrangement, telling Ford to say whatever he thought best and he would back him. When Ford met with the Mexican colonel, he listened to a long tirade translated by the adjutant. The colonel demanded to know by what right the Texans were on Mexican soil and whether they were going to pay for damages. When he paused for breath, Ford broke in as politely as possible and explained they had permission to enter Mexico. In turn, he demanded to know just how Mexican forces happened to be at La Mesa. Why did they not challenge? Why did they just start firing? Why were troops in ambush along the river? Why had the colonel brought six-hundred troops to a simple interview?

There was no answer to any of the questions. Instead, the colonel told Ford what would have happened to him had he been in command at La Mesa. In his version, few of the rangers would have answered another roll call. This was too much for the now disgusted Ford, who told the colonel he had two ranger companies against the colonel's several hundred men, but the U.S. troops would get out of the way and they would fight it out on the spot!

The generous offer was refused.

There was little doubt that the Mexican forces, whether regulars or the national guard, were sympathetic or actively cooperating with Cortina, and the horsemen driven away from La Mesa were undoubtedly his men. Despite their sympathies, the Mexican officers had no wish to start another fight and the Texans made no further advance. Several rangers had become lost in the dark the night before and were captured. The Mexicans released them, probably as a gesture of good will. The American forces stayed in Mexico for a day or so and returned to Texas.[69]

A Texan of the day could no more resist a dare than he could overlook a slur on his ability as a fighter, a characteristic that indirectly led to the next ranger action after hearing a rumor that the citizens of Reynosa had issued a challenging offer of thirty thousand dollars to any American forces who dared to enter their town. Long known as supporters of Cortina, the inhabitants of Reynosa had been active troublemakers in Texas. It was an offer the Texans could not refuse, but they had to wait.

Before they moved up to Reynosa, the two ranger companies and their army allies made an amazing sweep into Mexico, still after the elusive Cortina. They rode up to La Bolsa again then doubled back on rumors of Cortina's being at his ranch near Matamoros. In a little over forty-eight hours, the column covered close to 140 miles, riding cross-country along back roads. The march created a panic in the area; most Mexicans thought it was the beginning of another major invasion, and the citizens of Matamoros believed war had broken out. The Americans did not catch Cortina, but the unexpected march and the ease with which the American horsemen scouted as they pleased probably caused Cortina to abandon the Rio Grande and move inland near the mountains.[70]

After resting and refitting, Ford and Stoneman turned to the matter of Reynosa. There was no real thought of collecting the ludicrous "reward" for entering the place; their action was probably motivated more by a desire to humiliate the town for openly supporting the outlaws and for earlier raids. They probably thought they still had permission from Mexican authorities to cross the river after outlaws, but in later years Ford admitted he had considered the possibility that such a move might lead to war with Mexico and that such a conflict might have united the country and halted the sectional struggle taking place.[71]

At the time, most of the rangers and soldiers believed a number of Cortina's men were in Old Reynosa. Using little traveled trails, the rangers and soldiers traveled at night and camped during the day in hidden locations. Ford selected about eighty-five men from his two units and camped at a ranch thirty miles below Rio Grande City. The rangers rowed across the river in boats with their saddles and weapons, the horses swimming beside them.

Unfortunately, not all the rangers arrived in place around the town of Old Reynosa in time to block the escape of the outlaws. There was no use complaining about the way it turned out; instead, the Texans bought some needed supplies, took time out to enjoy a local *fandango*, and rode out for Reynosa the following morning. The U.S. soldiers were hidden just across the Rio Grande and were waiting to cross if needed; if a fight broke out in Reynosa, the rangers could expect prompt assistance.

The Texans entered the town from three directions: Ford led one party; Littleton commanded the detachment from his company, and Lieutenant Matthew Nolan and Lieutenant John Dix headed the third unit. They swept through Reynosa, riding along parallel streets, but it was a very tense few minutes because there were at least four-hundred armed Mexicans around the main plaza. As they rode slowly towards the center of the town, many of the Spanish speaking Texans taunted the snipers on the roof tops, inviting them to shoot if they dared. Nothing happened until the columns entered the plaza, where several of the Mexicans recognized Ford, yelled out who he was, and assured the others Ford had not come to rob them.

The Mexicans queried Ford as to why he had entered their town, and the ranger announced he had come for the thirty thousand dollars they had promised if he dared to run things as he had at Las Palmas and La Mesa. There was more talk, and the Mexicans finally escorted the rangers to the ferry after assurances they did not support Cortina. Both sides knew it was a blatant lie, but Ford had made his point and let it go.

When about half the rangers were back on the Texas side, Don Juan Treviño, one of the Mexican commanders, could not resist telling Ford how lucky he was the rangers had not started a fight earlier in the day. It was the wrong thing to say to the wrong man. Half of Ford's men were across the river but he offered to bring them back to test the accuracy of Treviño's statement. According the Ford, the "conversation took a different turn."

There seemed to have been a gentleman's agreement that Ford would give some warning if he decided to attack Reynosa, allowing time for the women and children to be moved to a safe location. Whether this was widely known is uncertain. It probably would not have mattered to the rangers, who were becoming bored the second night they were back on American soil. Littleton and some of the Texans decided to have some fun and constructed a "fort" on the bank opposite Reynosa. They set up a brick wall with a gun port and manufactured a cannon out of a log and a cart. A horn filled with powder and grease was exploded, sailing across the river in a fiery arc. Not surprisingly, the people in Reynosa had little sleep, expecting an attack at any moment.

An indignant emissary visited Ford next morning and accused him of bad faith. When the laughing Texans showed him the "artillery" he saw nothing humorous, grumbling the Texans were the most consummate rascals he had seen in all his travels. He may have been right! There was one actual exchange of fire during this time, with each side's blaming the other. Fortunately, there were no casualties other than several Mexicans' being wounded. Several days later, during a Mexican celebration, there was more firing. This seemed serious, and the U.S. soldiers rushed to the aid of their ranger friends. The sudden appearance of the troops, of whose presence they were completely unaware, was a major surprise to the Mexicans.[72]

The mixed U.S. Army and ranger force remained opposite Reynosa for a time but the Cortina trouble was over, at least for *that* decade.

Although the raiding and fight stopped along the Rio Grande for a time, diplomatic exchanges had just begun, and Washington and Mexico City would be involved in often heated discussions for years. The War Department sent Lieutenant Colonel Robert E. Lee to Texas as the new Department Commander with the additional duty of investigating the troubles in South Texas. A brevet colonel, Lee had been involved in checking Indians activities in north Texas, which delayed his arrival in San Antonio until February 19, 1860, but he assumed command the following day.[73] With a cavalry escort, he reached Eagle Pass on March 31 and moved down river, asking questions. On April 12, 1860, he made a blunt reply to Governor Andres Treviño's complaint about Ford's entrance into Reynosa.[74]

Ford rode to meet the new Department Commander at Edinburg. He wrote the meeting was cordial; Lee invited him to stay for supper and gently reproached him for entering Reynosa. "You should have sent a courier to inform them who you were," Lee suggested.[75]

For all his courtly manners and undoubted military talents, Lee had no real understanding of the dirty fighting on the Texas border. To his credit, he made every effort to find out the facts of the Cortina trouble and sent several sharp letters to various Mexican officials, demanding the Mexican government cease supporting Cortina.[76] There is nothing to suggest he made any effort to find out what the rangers had or had not done; he relied on Major Heintzelman's final report for that part of the story. In the major's report on March 1, he arrived in Brownsville with 117 men, took over the demoralized

Texas Rangers, and routed Cortina's bandits near Rio Grande City on December 27, 1859. Thereafter the bandits disintegrated rapidly.[77] In his report of department activities, Lee wrote much the same version.[78] Lee mentioned a few ranger commanders but inferred they were commanded by Heintzelman and that the U.S. soldiers did the fighting. Even though he listed the casualties, he did not find anything odd about two slightly wounded soldiers, listed by name, as opposed to one ranger death and sixteen wounded Texans. In time, Lee's version became the official account of how Cortina was beaten, and by the 1920s the army histories did not even mention the rangers.[79]

Ford must not have seen Heintzelman's report or that of Lee, because there is no reference to them in his *Memoirs*. At the time, he had things to keep him busy other than defending his reputation. Action in the valley was over, but Governor Houston had other troubles to consider. On March 24, 1860, he sent Ford a letter informing him of the appointment of George McKnight as commissioner with special orders from the governor. Ford and Littleton were to march to Goliad and await further instructions. The same day, Houston notified Colonel Lee that McKnight was on the way to confer with him and make such disposition of state troops as deemed necessary. The same day, Houston gave McKnight orders making him a commissioner with full authority to muster out any and all state troops then in service. If there appeared to be any need for rangers, the commissioner could muster in such troops as Colonel Lee thought necessary. Rangers in service would go to Goliad for disposition. McKnight was to take all state arms and property to Goliad, but only enough rations would be moved to feed the rangers on the march to Goliad.[80]

McKnight's instructions contained Houston's usual concern about controlling waste and expenses, but the rangers received the mistaken impression he had been sent to keep them from stealing. Ford mentions in passing this caused some ill will but that it did not prevent McKnight from receiving courteous attention.

As a farewell gesture, the people in Brownsville somewhat hastily arranged a farewell dinner for Ford, which Lee attended as a guest. For reasons unknown, Major Heintzelman was not invited. He noted the omission in his journal, stating he left in the afternoon of the party as he was already packed for movement to his new station, but it must have rankled him because he noted he thought he had done something for the town and no one had recognized it. He did not care to stay for the event that evening, though "I very much esteem Major Ford." In the next several days, Ford, Lee and Heintzelman traveled together part of the way to Banquete, where they separated.[81]

As soon as possible, the two ranger companies marched up to Goliad and were discharged, final pay rolls being certified by McKnight on May 17 for Ford and May 18 for Littleton.[82]

There is a final footnote to this story. Commissioner McKnight took his instructions from the governor as gospel and, when some of the ranger officers offered to help in the turn-in of property, he refused their assistance. Later, leaving Goliad, Ford noticed many of the rangers were still armed. One told him that when McKnight accepted a weapon, he handed it to one of his helpers who placed it in the front of the wagon. A waiting ex-ranger then slipped the weapon out of the rear of the wagon and returned it to the man who had just turned it in![83]

The bloody days along the Rio Grande thus ended in another ranger prank, marking the last of Ford's ranger service. Old Rip rode back to Austin and into the approaching storm that would result in a colonelcy with the Confederacy. And for a time, Sam Houston could forget Cortina and concentrate on the Indian problem in the north.

—8—
SAM HOUSTON
AND THE INDIANS

Sam Houston became Governor of Texas in time to inherit the Cortina mess along the Rio Grande. His eagerness to clean up this trouble and discharge Ford's rangers was largely because he had major Indian problems in the north. As suggested earlier, his election was partially due to frontier dissatisfaction with Runnels' defense against Indian attacks. Houston had always been a champion of Indian rights, a position that had hurt him in the past. Now, in the first days of 1860 and his new administration, he was faced with renewed Indian attacks along the northern and western frontier. He expressed this dilemma in his first message to the Texas Legislature.

> The office of the Executive falls into my hands at a peculiar period in our history as a state...a considerable portion of our state bordering on the Rio Grande River is in a state of turmoil and war, our frontier is unprotected and harassed by Indians....[1]

Houston outlined the events of the Cortina affair up to the time of his message. He continued by noting that even though no appropriation had been made to pay for defending the frontier against Indian raids, he had used his constitutional powers to raise ranger companies to protect the settlers. A bill had come to his desk, "An Act for the protection of the frontier," outlining how companies would be organized and the rates of pay, but it provided no money for payment. He sarcastically noted he already had the power to form units—what he needed was money to pay them![2]

In such manner, Houston took over the old Texas problem of

the defense of its citizens without having any funds to pay for their defense . Whatever he may have once thought about Indians, the governor made every effort to protect his people, and during 1860 more ranger units were raised than in any other year in Texas history.[3] While trying to sort out the conflicting stories about the Cortina fighting, Houston was faced with a series of Indian attacks all along the frontier. After raids were made within fifty miles of Austin[4], Houston sent the following instructions:

Executive Department, Austin, January 20, 1860.
To Captain W. C. Dalrymple, Commanding 1st Company
Sir: You will proceed with as little delay as possible and make your headquarters at some point on the frontier, at least five miles from the settlements, and between Fish Creek in Cook County, and Big Wichita, at such points as you may think best to give the greatest amount of protection to the inhabitants. You will divide your command in three divisions, making three stations, or more, should you think proper for the protection and comfort of your command and such fencing as you may think proper for the security of your horses.

You will see that daily patrols pass and repass from post to post, when the weather, or the state of your command will permit. Horses lost in action and killed by the enemy, are not to be paid for, nor the loss of arms paid for.

In the police and the arrangement of your encampments or stations, you will, if possible, secure the health and comfort of the troops. You will regularly detail and mount guards, and besides constant vigilance and care, the moral tone of your command will be a subject which is particularly confided to your authority.

No horse racing, or gambling is to be permitted or practiced; nor are any intoxicating liquors of any kind to be brought within your camp or camps, or used. Nor will you permit any person or persons to bring nearer than five miles, any spirits of any kind, or sell same to a member, or members of your command.

You will not permit more than four men to be absent from your command at any time on leave or furlough.

It is impossible to regulate at this distance from the theater of your command all the details, and there must necessarily be a given to render the command as efficient as possible.

And I enjoin upon you, Captain, and the troops to use all means in your power, not only to give the protection so necessary for the safety of the lives and property of our frontier inhabitants, but to pay an especial regard to their persons, rights and property, and to see that no molestation takes place at anything belonging to the inhabitants.

Monthly reports and returns of the state of condition of your command will be made to the Executive Department at this place, with such information on the state of the frontier as you may deem important.

You can extend or contract your lines of observation as you may think the state of the frontier requires, and will best afford it protection.

You are authorized to select six good Mexican guides, to be regularly enrolled in your company with pay not to exceed that of privates.

You are authorized to procure a blacksmith with suitable tools and muster him into your company as a private, with such extra compensation as is allowed by the regulations of the United States army.

Any member guilty of intoxication or insubordination will be dismissed without honorable discharge.

                                        Sam Houston

Basically the same order was sent to Ed Burleson in Hays County on January 14, 1860, and to John H. Conner on January 13.[5] Dalrymple had his company formed by January 14; Conner was organized by January 20, and Burleson was ready on January 30.[6] While not mentioned in their orders, the time of service was to be one year.[7]

There was no trouble enlisting the companies. At the time, the standard mounted company had sixty privates, with officers and non-commissioned officers bringing the total to seventy. Conner found sixty privates; Dalrymple enlisted sixty-five and Burleson sixty-nine.[8] Each captain had a blacksmith, a desirable addition since the companies were to operate far from any support facilities. Although not specified, each company had a surgeon; there was no quibble over these unauthorized medical men when the companies were paid off and discharged.

Houston's instructions regarding drinking are of interest because they became standard in later years. Rangers have traditionally been considered wild, romantic, hard living and without control or discipline, but historically this has not been the case. They were never under the rigid control of an army unit, but most all ranger captains understood the need for some form of control and standards of conduct. Although standards varied from the strict drilling and discipline of Ford to the overly loose control of Tobin, they were always understood. Drunken men did not win battles, and absent rangers did not scout or fight. There are numerous notations in earlier muster rolls showing men dishonorably discharged, but Houston was the first governor to spell out in written instructions what was expected of the rangers.

These three units kept busy, even though they did not have the pitched battles of earlier days. Remarks on the rolls show numerous scouts, detached service, and fatigue duty. Two men in Dalrymple's company died, evidently from natural causes. The rolls show that only Conner had obtained the guides allowed by Houston, seven rather than the four authorized, none Hispanic. There are obvious Spanish surnames on the various rolls, but none are identified as guides. The three units were formed in counties with small Hispanic populations, but the matter of the few Hispanic enrollments is of importance only in relation to whether or not Houston had a plan to invade Mexico, as discussed later in this chapter.

Houston soon found more rangers were needed. Raiding beyond Bell County brought about the formation of numerous "Minute Companies." Lieutenant Robert M. White of Bell County was called on to form a twenty-five man detachment on February 13, as was Lieutenant Dixon Walker for the protection of Erath County.[9] Detachment muster rolls indicate these units were formed on February 20 and February 25.

While the organization of many small units had been criticized earlier, Houston evidently saw it as the only way to combat the extensive raids during early 1860. On February 21 he authorized each county to form a minute company of no more than twenty men, commanded by a lieutenant. They were to look to the next legislature for pay. A general order on March 9 allowed the chief justice of each county to field a fifteen-man unit.[10] Houston went into exhaustive detail in his instructions for these small detachments. As always, he was explicit about economy and safeguarding state funds and property. For the first time, a unit commander had to post a bond to cover arms and supplies issued to his men. Other details are of no general interest, but there was a final admonition that caused troubles later; Houston specifically stated all recovered property would be returned to known owners and that any ranger receiving compensation for returning property would be discharged.

The governor must have placed considerable faith in these detachments. He managed to obtain one-hundred Colt revolvers for their use, as well as other arms, and saw that ammunition was made available. Later, he reported fifteen of the detachments were formed. There are nine muster rolls in the surviving archives which, from the dates of service, numbers and rank of the commander, seem to be from his March 9 order.

He seemed satisfied these detachments, in addition to the ranger companies already in service, could defend the frontier. When a friend offered the services of a ranger company for duty in Tarrant County, Houston politely declined. He stated the settlers did not want people from the sheltered, interior counties coming to their rescue. Houston mentioned the special detachments, plus other troops, would make a force of 730 men to guard against Indian raids. However, he added this ominous paragraph:

> The whole amount of money in the treasury sub-
> ject to the frontier defense for the next two years is
> 91,537. 37$. This will not furnish the regular compa-
> nies with supplies. The troops called out by the
> Executive must be fed. For their pay they will have to
> look to the Legislature.[11]

Pay or no pay, the various detachments did the best they could. Lieutenant Dixon Walker wrote Houston that conditions had become calmer since he first reported, and that there had been no Indian sign in the past ten days. However, he needed forage—and everything else. Still, he noted, the Indians had stopped using their regular trails. He had "two little runs in and we got ther beef & butcher knife the material they made paints & several other thing The brush saved them."[12]

Life in these ranger units was harsh under normal conditions. When there was no forage for the horses, or food for the men unless they could buy it themselves or hunt, life was miserable. When Walker reported for April 1860, he listed himself and five men for duty. Two were sick in Stephenville, nine were on a ten-day furlough and seven had left the service.[13]

During March 1860, Houston also formed a forty-eight man ranger company in Atascosa County. He chose Peter Tumlinson for this job, and the old timer, barely out of service along the Rio Grande chasing Cortina, came back to defend the country between the Frio and the Rio Grande.[14] Economy had become almost an obsession with the governor. He told Tumlinson if he could not "obtain supplies by regular contract, you will have to provide for the men, returning vouchers to this Department as best you may, always keeping an eye to the strictest economy and the greatest protection of the frontier."[15]

Tumlinson formed a new company and was on station in Sabinal, from where he reported to the governor on April 24, 1860, with his allotted forty privates, three sergeants, three corporals, plus two lieutenants, two guides and a surgeon. They were all well mounted and armed, with ten to fifteen shots a man indicating that every ranger had at least one revolver; many of them had two as well as a rifle, and possibly a shotgun or extra single-shot pistols.

The rangers were active; Tumlinson split the company into fifteen-man patrols to scout all over his territory, paying close attention to the headwaters of the major streams and natural Indian trails into the settlements. They found no Indian signs.[16]

The constant ranger patrols discouraged Comanche raids, even if no fighting contacts were made, and settlers were quick to notice the change. Citizens in Bandera County petitioned Houston to retain Tumlinson in service and send him back where he had been originally stationed. After describing conditions before the rangers came, their letter continued:

> . . . if the Ranging protection is taken from us We must leave with them for we have had no peace for a great while until Capt. Tumlinson came to our relief with his mounted Rangers which for two months he has continually scoured our country - and we have felt safe for the first time. Ther has been several Indians trails pass through a remote portion of our country but never venture in the settlements since the Rangers have been here.
>
> And from the continued Scouts Capt Tumlinson has kept up we prefer him to any protection that could be sent.[17]

Even if there were no Indian fights, the constant patrolling kept raiding parties away. Citizens in Lampasas County also wrote Houston to retain their ranger company in service, informing the governor that the peace they had enjoyed was due to Captain Moses Hughes and his rangers.[18]

All of Texas' governors had taken a role in organizing ranger companies, as well as trying to find money to pay them, but Sam Houston went further and tried to direct them. On March 1, he sent Ed Burleson to penetrate Indian country to the Cedar Mountains and headwater of the Wichitas where it was believed Indian thieves had a large herd of stolen horses. Houston instructed Burleson to leave enough men to protect the settlements and to call on Conner for twenty-five rangers to augment his expedition. If feasible, he could call on Dalrymple for a like number, providing it did not delay him. Houston gave Burleson some discretion to use his own judgement once in the field, but on one matter he did not give any leeway and directed that, "If you take any white men associated with the Indians, you will know how to treat them as traitors."[19]

Burleson, who had waited a long time to be a company commander, wasted no time moving out and sent back a dispatch saying he was on the march to the Wichita Mountains with seventy-five men, plus twenty-five from Conner's company. Unfortunately, he had to lodge a complaint about Conner's grudging cooperation, saying the other captain had acted in a manner unbecoming an officer and a gentleman. He promised a full report when he returned in twenty-five days, which was the amount of rations he carried.

There was an interesting request at the end of the dispatch; Burleson asked to be sent to the border if war broke out with Mexico. He reminded the governor he knew the country well and spoke the language.[20] In March of 1860 the trouble with Cortina was not yet over, and talk of war was common in Texas, even reaching Burleson's rangers stationed far in front of the settlements. On March 21, Houston published a proclamation denouncing any such invasion and citing the negative effects it would have on diplomatic relations and a treaty then before the U.S. Senate for ratification. He went on to call attention to the sufferings on the frontier. Houston said in so many words that if men wanted to fight, let them turn to their own bleeding and suffering fellow citizens, who cried out for help along the frontier.[21]

The last thing Houston needed was a war with Mexico. In addition to doing everything he could to wind up the problems in the valley, discharge Ford's rangers, and concentrate on the frontier Indians, he had troubles with his own rangers, or feared he might. Burleson's complaints about Conner's not wanting to split his company must have struck a nerve with the governor, because a few days earlier he had written Conner and informed him that serious charges had been preferred against him by several citizens who claimed the rangers in his company had charged for returning stolen horses. There was a claim that one horse had been bought back by its owner for thirty dollars and others repurchased for fees of five to eight dollars a head. There was another charge that liquor had been brought into the ranger camp by Lieutenant Gillett for the private use of Doctor Todd.[22]

Both allegations violated specific, written instructions for ranger conduct and discipline. The use of whiskey in camp was serious enough, but the allegation that the rangers were demanding money to return stolen property must have infuriated the governor. This action struck at the very foundation of ranger honor. Fortunately, the story did not develop as alleged.

With Conner absent on a scout, Lieutenant James S. Gillett replied immediately to the governor's letter. He informed Houston the company kept full records, which he had examined and inclosed a copy for the governor. About forty-five dollars had been given to the company as a voluntary contribution to defray expenses the rangers had incurred in caring for recovered animals. The rangers had recaptured twenty-three horses and kept them for two weeks while owners were being found. Gillett explained most citizens took their horses home without paying anything, voluntary or otherwise. The allegation that five to eight dollars had been charged per horse was false and malicious.

As to the liquor, the lieutenant admitted he had brought a sealed package addressed to Doctor Todd to the camp. Since he and the doctor were not speaking, he had no idea what was inside the package, only that he had brought it to camp after picking it up from a druggist. He had promised to place the box in the medical tent until the doctor returned to camp.[23]

It was a commendable defense for a junior officer, and later investigation showed it to be true. In the meantime, Conner returned from his scout and requested a short leave of absence to attend to urgent business in Austin.[24] Evidently it was granted.

Houston must have been relieved to read Gillett's explanation of the charges made against the rangers. However, he was not a man to take much on faith, and he had a trusted friend make an independent investigation. Talks with an eyewitness to the return of the horses disclosed the rangers had said only that if anyone wanted to contribute for taking care of the recovered animals they could do so. As Gillett wrote, most of the owners had taken their horses and left.[25] The matter of Doctor Todd's whiskey was never explained.

Conner kept busy, even with part of his company away with Burleson. These men returned on April 11, their horses worn down after having been away most of a month. Conner reported this to

Houston, mentioning he was going out again on a scout. His lieutenants had been busy, but all they had found were old foot tracks on the Colorado. Conner believed some foot Indians were below him, but there was not much that could be done until they actually stole something.[26]

Conner's company was disbanded May 8, 1860.[27] He had at least recovered some stolen horses, and there seems little doubt that his extensive patrolling in a five-county area had stopped serious raiding. Burleson had much the same record. His expedition to the Wichita Mountains resulted in no fighting, but another strike into Comanche territory must have been unsettling to the Indians. For a time, the Indian threat was reduced to small groups of foot Indians trying to steal horses. Houston credited the various detachments for eliminating, or seriously reducing, Indian attacks.[28]

The easiest way to tell the ranger story in 1860 is to follow certain events, leaders or units as they played their part in history. It was a busy year, and often several commanders were active at the same time. Old Sam Houston was down in Austin tugging at all the strings and planning major strikes while desperately trying to handle emergency conditions with his county detachments. It is clear his authorization of the small units for local defense for a short term of service was almost a political act, although the detachments did some good work.

The governor was thinking of a long range plan to strike north of the Red River into Comanche hunting grounds. It was fairly well established that foot raiders brought back stolen horses and sold them to traders north of the Red. Houston proposed a major expedition to find and punish the traders.[29]

M.T. Johnson of Tarrant County was selected to command the force, with the rank of colonel. On March 17, 1860, he was authorized to form five ranger companies,[30] which he accomplished by mid April when the units began marching to Fort Belknap where they were joined by Burleson and Dalrymple.

One of the five companies was formed in Waco with J.M. Smith as captain. Lawrence Sullivan Ross was 1st lieutenant. Young Ross had recovered from the severe wound received in the expedition with Van Dorn and was willing to try his luck again, but his service during the earlier strike was not to count for much when they reached the frontier settlements. Feeling still ran high against Ross' father and against rangers in general because of their presumed defense of the agency Indians. When one lady learned Ross was the son of Agent Ross, she screamed she hoped the Indians killed him and his company![31]

In the voting for regimental officers, Captain Smith was elected lieutenant colonel and Ross became company commander. Although he was sick during much of the campaign, he did acquire valuable experience commanding a ranger company.[32] There were, however, not many positive lessons from Johnson's expedition; it is unfortunate that the largest concentration of ranger forces in the decade was not better led. The basic objective—to punish crooked traders—may have been laudable, but there was no intelligence to go on and no sound plan. Compounding everything was Colonel Johnson, who was initially more interested in romance than rangering. Towards the end of May he placed Smith in command and left to get married! He explained to the governor he would only be a short time, about three weeks, and asked him to understand.[33]

With or without Johnson, the rangers made an effort to locate Indians and covered more territory than any force had scouted before. Even Johnson was active once he returned, leading a major force after Kickapoos during July and August.[34] Much of the country between the Red River and the Arkansas had been burned off, and marching through this arid terrain was extremely difficult. The rangers, at one time or another, went up to Fort Cobb in the Indian Territory, where they were assured none of the reservation Indians had been raiding into Texas. The scout after Kickapoos was futile; the Indians had been alerted and had fled to Fort Arbuckle where U.S. Army officers gave the rangers a cordial welcome but told the Texans the Indians were under their protection.

Captain Peter F. Ross, no relation to L.S. Ross, led a spy company. He took a number of Tonkaway guides and scouted along the Canadian River, which flowed through dry terrain largely unknown even to his guides. The water in the Canadian was apparently undrinkable, because the rangers had to scatter to find water and were surprised several times by Indian hit-and-run attacks. The scattered patrols finally reassembled with nothing to show other than some lost mounts. They finally returned to their base camp with many rangers on foot.[35]

The expedition stayed out longer than was militarily sensible. Johnson hated to give up, even after the friendly Indian scouts quit and returned home.[36] If James Pike can be believed, the command was close to mutiny several times. In his account, they did have some actual contact with Indian camps and suffered some casualties.[37]

Remembrances years later, however, do not always agree with the contemporary reports of the period. Johnson had collected most of his men at Camp Radziminski by the end of July when he reported to Houston. He included various reports by subordinates on their scouts and concluded there was no chance of finding any large Indian camps. They had all retreated north and west, far beyond the contemplated limits of the expedition. Johnson made no mention of any major moves by the command.[38]

It was clear the great venture was at an end. By August 4, when he sent Johnson additional instructions, Houston had abandoned any hope of accomplishing anything.[39] He said that he had delayed replying to Johnson's last dispatch for two weeks in hopes something positive might be forthcoming from the colonel, stating that, "You seem in your letter to have no plan digested for future operations. The troops cannot remain inactive at such expense to the Government."

He instructed Johnson to send the companies back to their home counties and discharge them. The companies led by Burleson and Dalrymple were to be formed into a battalion, with a major to be elected as commander. The new command would be sent on a campaign along the Salt Fork of the Colorado, across the Concho. He told Johnson that he hoped to achieve something out of the campaign by this move. Houston also included instructions for the twenty-one thousand rations sent to Fort Belknap for the abortive expedition.

The same day Houston sent instructions to Burleson and Dalrymple concerning his decision to form their companies into a battalion.[40] Both ranger commands remained in service until the following year, though there is no record to show what they might have accomplished.

Houston must have been bitterly disappointed at spending so much money for nothing and possibly risking the loss of thousands of costly rations. He did not make any public comment, but he did send Johnson a sarcastic letter over a month after he thought he had given Johnson his final instructions.

> Executive Department, September 12, 1860.
> Colonel M. T. Johnson, Commanding Texas Rangers
>   Sir: Lieutenant Hammet with dispatches from Captain Dalrymple arrived here last evening. He brought none from you. Under other circumstances I might have been surprised, as it is, I am not.
>   Such a length of time since my orders of August 4th, and nothing thus far has been done. You will immediately upon receipt of this order carry into execution that portion of my orders of August 4th relating to the disbanding of the troops raised by you.

Houston concluded, saying he had just learned Captain Thomas J. Johnson had declined the command of a ranger company to be based near Fort Belknap and had offered the new unit to L.S. Ross.[41]

In his directive to Ross, Houston authorized him to form a more-or-less standard ranger company—sixty privates with three lieutenants, four sergeants and four corporals—to be stationed at Fort Belknap. A considerable part of the letter concerned the selection of twenty trusted men to go with all dispatch to Belknap and guard the rations stored there. Ross was allowed to distribute enough rations to Johnson's men to get them to their homes. Houston gave Ross the usual instructions about chasing Indians, and he added that the ranger was to hold himself in readiness at all times to support civil authorities in cases of resistance to the laws.[42]

Ross was not Houston's first choice for the new ranger company, and just why he selected him is unknown. The young man was twenty-two and had made a name with Van Dorn in 1858 as a volunteer leading the reserve Indians, but his experience as a company commander during the Johnson Expedition certainly did nothing to suggest he might make a ranger leader. It was true he was a recent college graduate, undoubtedly the only one among ranger captains of the time, but this would not qualify him for office. Houston must have made part of his choice because of Ross' father. Whatever his reasons, Sam Houston made one of his better officer choices when he picked young L.S. Ross.

The new captain wasted no time forming his company. His muster roll shows some men enlisted as early as September 22, but most enlisted on October 3, 1860, the official mustering-in date. A few others came in on October 13 and 18.[43] Ross signed on three officers, four sergeants, four corporals and a blacksmith but could find only forty-four privates. Of these men, seven would be discharged, three would desert and two would be killed, but along the way, they contributed a noted chapter in ranger annals.

Ross could not have dreamed that an event that began two years before he was born would involve him on the Pease River a few weeks in the future. In May 1836 a Comanche war party had attacked Parker's Fort near present day Waco, killing several members of the Parker family and capturing a little girl and her brother. The Parker family searched for the children for years, but Cynthia Ann Parker grew up among the Comanches and eventually became the squaw of one of the chiefs, Peta Nacona. Her brother was raised as a Comanche brave. There were several reported sightings of the children, but by the time Ross was organizing his company it is doubtful if anyone believed Cynthia Ann was still alive.[44]

Twenty-four years after the Parker Massacre, Ross made a base camp near Fort Belknap and was soon scouting. November was a relatively quiet month in the beginning, but Indian attacks increased as the days passed. Parker, Young, Palo Pinto and Jack counties were struck again and again, and Houston began receiving appeals for help, calling his attention to stock losses and murder by the Indians. On December 6 he wrote Ross that he had authorized two new detachments of twenty-five men to help defend the frontier. The rangers would report to Ross and be under his command.[45] James Barry of Brazos County and Thomas Stockton of Young County were designated to lead the detachments.[46] Faced with a growing emergency, Houston called on A.B. Burleson to form a standard seventy-man company.[47] None of these official ranger units was formed in time to help Ross, and only a company of Palo Pinto County volunteers, commanded by Jack Cureton, reached the ranger camp in time to take part in the scout against the Comanches.

Houston wrote Ross another letter on December 19 telling him of ordering the two detachments to join his command. He expressed an opinion that large numbers of Indians intended to winter in Texas and every effort must be made to expel them. Any Indian south of the Red River was to be considered an enemy unless escorted by soldiers or bearing dispatches.[48]

Ross did not receive this correspondence in time to make any difference; the question of where Indians belonged had already been well established. When the ranger captain returned to his camp from a scout, he found the place in an uproar; some civilian volunteers had been tracking a raiding party and located a Comanche camp up on the Pease River. Ross decided to go after them, but after he left behind enough rangers for local protection, his company was reduced to around forty men. Even with Cureton's volunteers, this was not enough. Ross went to Captain N.G. Evans, the commander of the U.S. forces at Camp Cooper with whom he had become friends during the Van Dorn expedition, and asked for his help.

Without too much regard for regulations, Evans detached Sergeant John W. Spangler and twenty troopers of Company H, 2nd Cavalry. Spangler had also been with Van Dorn.[49] Ross started north with his forty men, twenty of the army's soldiers, and possibly seventy civilians. It was an uneasy alliance; the civilian volunteers came from an area plagued with hostile attacks by Indians they believed to be from the reservations, and they distrusted both the rangers and the soldiers.

The rangers began to think they might have good hunting on this trip when they ran into large herds of buffalo moving south. Either a large hunting party was above them or a major Indian camp. Ross said in later years this was on December 18. The rangers and the cavalrymen were considerably ahead of Cureton and his volunteers at this time. The civilian horses were not in good shape and were lagging far behind. The cold weather was also taking a toll on the animals. Ross kept pushing, moving his mixed force along the low ground near the Pease River. The country was prairie land in which the only distinctive terrain features were a few small sand hills. That particular day, it was not only cold but extremely windy. Most of the time, blowing sand severely limited visibility.

Ross kept atop the crests of the hills where possible, trying to see through the flying sand. Low as they were, the rises offered the only commanding view of the countryside, and the ranger tried to spot any enemy forces while keeping his own men hidden. On one hilltop, Ross found fresh tracks. Certain they were near Indians, Ross rode towards the highest rise in the area from where he was able to see an Indian village no more than two hundred yards away!

The heavy weather saved the ranger. The thick clouds of blowing sand concealed Ross from the Indians. Through brief breaks in the blowing dust, Ross saw the village was near a stream next to which the Indians were busily dismantling the tepees and preparing to move. He turned and rode down the slope away from the Indians and galloped back to find his men.

Ross was able to signal his column, and they rode up to the shelter of the hills unobserved. The ranger had a decision to make: attack or wait for Cureton and his seventy men. He was certainly outnumbered, but if he waited the Comanches could easily finish breaking camp and vanish in the sandstorm. Despite his youth, he immediately made the right choice. He sent Spangler and the twenty soldiers around the hills to maneuver behind the Comanches and block their retreat. Taking his rangers, he rode directly toward the slowly moving Indians, now leaving the abandoned campsite.

Once again, the wind-blown sand concealed the rangers until they were almost among the Indians. The opening rounds of the fight dropped several Comanches, and several others in the lead broke and started to run but collided with the soldiers. The shots from the army's weapons caused more casualties and scattered the Indians. In his later accounts of the fight, Ross did not divide the battle into specific incidents or phases, but other accounts mentioned that a number of Comanche braves turned back after the first panic and tried to stop the rangers long enough for the women and children and all the animals and camp equipment to escape.[50] This was standard Comanche practice.

A small band ran into a ravine, hoping to hide or slip through the rangers and soldier lines, but were turned back. Some of the camp dogs took part, snapping and barking and finally forcing the attackers to shoot them.

The main fight took place when other braves returning to their camp ran into the advancing rangers. Several of the Comanches had firearms and for a time halted the Texans' advance in a gallant battle.

Slowly, however, the Indians began to fall back as the rangers rode up and began a concentrated fire into the Comanches, who had dismounted and were using their horses as shields. All the Comanches were bundled in buffalo robes, and none of the rangers had any idea some of the fighters were women. One large warrior, yelling commands, suddenly ran for one of the uninjured horses and pulled up another Indian behind him, dashing at the nearest ranger in the closing circle. The warrior, or a Comanche near him, shot an arrow at Lieutenant M.W. Sommerville, who dropped down to avoid the shaft. It was all the mounted pair needed and they rode through the gap, followed by another Comanche who had mounted in the confusion.

Trying to halt the Comanches now running in all directions, Ross sent twelve rangers after some of the Indians. They stayed together, fearing ambush if they split up, and kept to the ravines and low ground, following a set of two pony tracks that had broken away from the main column. Eventually the rangers spotted a large Comanche camp in the distance that was apparently being abandoned because the tepees were being hastily taken down. It seemed evident the two riders had alerted the other camp to the ranger attack. Once certain the Indians were running, the rangers turned back to report to Ross.

He was in a fight miles away in the sand and dirt. Each combatant fought what was close, what he could see, and many individual and small group battles were taking place on the prairie and in the numerous draws and ravines along the stream that emptied into Pease River. Whether Ross was part of the circle about the trapped Comanches or rode up just as the two riders broke clear is not clear, but he and Lieutenant Tom Kelliher did see the two Comanches running and started after them. The four horses soon left behind the sounds of the fight and galloped across the prairie. Kelliher was in the lead, riding a fine horse, and steadily gained on the trailing Comanche. After a mile, he was so close he leaned over to try a revolver shot. The Comanche must have turned in time to see the weapon, because the rider suddenly jerked the pony to a halt and held out a small baby!

Ross, riding up on the other side of this Indian pony, was still trying for a clear shot until he saw the rider was a woman. He yelled for the lieutenant to stay with the prisoner and continued after the other pair of Indians, gaining on them even after the slight halt. The grass fed ponies of the Comanches could not outrun the ranger horses, and the other animal was carrying two riders although Ross was not aware of this at the time. After another half mile, Ross was close enough to see that there were two Comanches on the pony. Closing to within twenty yards, he fired a shot from his Colt revolver. The ball went through the rear Comanche and struck the other brave's shield, worn Comanche style across his back.

Struck in the heart, the rear rider died instantly still clutching the forward rider about the waist and dragging him from the horse. Ross galloped by, noting the Comanche had slung his shield around and was fitting an arrow to his bow! Before the ranger could stop or draw aside, the Indian hit his horse with the arrow. The injured animal, more startled than crippled, began bucking and started to fall, almost throwing Ross. While the ranger struggled to keep his seat and control the horse, the Comanche was able to loose other arrows. Ross, barely escaping this shower, fired another round in desperation and struck the brave in the right elbow, disabling the man. Ross managed to quiet his horse, finding the wound was not serious, and turned back to the Comanche, still trying to draw his bow. The ranger came closer and shot the Comache twice, each round hitting in the body. For the first time, Ross obtained a good view of the man, noting he was unusually large. Bundled in buffalo robes, he must have seemed a giant. Despite two major wounds, he refused to fall although it was evident he was dying.

There was a small tree close by, the only break on the endless prairie. Still carrying a lance in his left hand, the Comanche staggered over, leaned against the trunk, and began singing his death song. When Ross dismounted and came close, he tried to stab him with the lance. A few minutes earlier, the ranger had been trying to kill the Comanche, but now he could not bring himself to fire the last round.

Two of the rangers galloped up with Ross' servant, Antonio Martinez, who had been a Comanche prisoner for many years after his family was murdered by a raiding party. He spoke the language and knew the wounded Comanche. He had been the man's slave for several years and identified him as Peta Nacona. With no hesitation, Conner walked over and fired both barrels of his shotgun into the

Indian. While collecting the dead brave's weapons and equipment, they discovered the other body was that of a young woman.

Ross and Antonio rode back to find Kelliher and the Comanche prisoner. The lieutenant was disgusted at exhausting his horse to capture a dirty squaw, until he obtained a closer look at the woman and discovered she had blue eyes. Despite her clothing, she was not Indian. When the other two rangers rode up they casually mentioned they had scalped the dead Indian by the tree, an act Ross naturally neglected to mention in his various accounts of the battle.

The woman must have guessed what they were talking about and made them take her to the bodies of the two dead Comanches. She dismounted and walked about the corpse of the man, calling out "Nacona" several times. She paid her respects to the dead woman, as Comanche wives did under such circumstances. Antonio recognized what she was doing—one wife showing courtesy to another wife. They could not persuade her to leave the spot until warning she would make them kill her if she did not leave.

The scattered rangers began riding back, bringing in captured horses, weapons and pack animals loaded with smoked meat, camp supplies and trophies of every description. The arms and shield of the dead chief were collected to be sent to Governor Houston for deposit in the State Archives.[51] During this assembly period, the men with Cureton finally rode up and were bitterly disappointed at not sharing in the plunder.

That night Ross and Antonio talked with the captured squaw, and the ranger began to wonder if she could be the legendary Cynthia Ann Parker. She talked easily enough with Antonio about her life with the Comanches, but she did not remember any English or how she came to be with them. While the various ranger groups were assembling at the rendezvous point, Ross and several others had found an Indian boy about eight or nine years old. Once he was sure he would not be killed, the lad was at ease in his new surroundings. It was not so with the woman, even after Antonio repeatedly assured her she was safe. It finally became clear she was not worried for her safety, or that of her daughter, but for the safety of her two boys who had left the Comanche column just before the fighting began.

Before they returned to their camp at Belknap, Ross was almost certain she was Cynthia Ann and sent her and the child to Camp

Cooper where army wives could look after them. Antonio went along to interpret. At the same time Ross notified her uncle, Isaac Parker, who lived near Weatherford. In a meeting with him, she remembered her name and was definitely identified as the missing Cynthia Ann. Romantic fiction would be able to find a happy ending to this story, but reality is not always a rainbow. Cynthia Ann never did adjust to a life her relatives considered civilized. They made every effort to help her, but she had lived too long with the Comanches. Her daughter soon died and Cynthia Ann, who was about thirty-four when found, lived only until 1864. She never knew that one of her sons would be Quanah Parker, the last free Comanche chief.

The fight and scattering of Nacona's Comanche band added to the reputation of young Ross. The aggressive actions of the rangers did much to erase the hard feelings among many of the frontier settlers. At the time, and for many years, Ross was known as the ranger who killed Peta Nacona, and thus he became a part of Texas history.[52] As late as 1882 or 1883, Quanah Parker, by then nationally known, refused to visit the site along Mule Creek near the Pease River, saying his father had been killed there. A few years later he suddenly changed his story, explaining his father had not been killed in the fight and that he and his brother were not the ones the rangers tracked to the second Indian camp. He started a controversy that lasts to this day, with various possible identifications of the man killed that harsh, winter day. The doubt rest solely on Quanah's word and on the naive belief that an Indian would never lie.[53] Whoever was killed and scalped that day cannot be identified beyond a shadow of a doubt, but Peta Nacona was never seen or heard from again. He had been a commanding figure, unusually large for a Comanche, and if he had appeared anywhere, he would have been noticed.

The death of Peta Nacona is not the only historical puzzle of this period. Some historians have seen Sam Houston's calling out of rangers in large numbers as something other than defense against Indians. Walter Prescott Webb believed the old man contemplated an invasion of Mexico.[54] He cites the fact that Houston wrote the U.S. Secretary of War and asked for thousands of weapons and cavalry accouterments and offered to raise a five-thousand man force to defend the borders![55] It was probably no surprise when Secretary

John B. Floyd declined the offer.

Houston kept after Floyd for funds and troops, extolling the virtues of the rangers and their ability to fight on the frontier.[56] Just how any of this figured into a plan to invade Mexico is unclear. On the surface, it appears that his actions were no more than the usual proposals of various Texas governors to obtain money and troops to protect exposed settlements. Towards the end of 1860, on November 28, he wrote Floyd again with a plea for a battalion of rangers to be called into federal service. He hastened to add he was not disparaging the U.S. Army; it was just they were not always suited to the task. Once again, he pointed out the special skills of the rangers.[57]

When these various documents are examined, it is easy to make a case for frontier defense, nothing more. Houston repeatedly claimed he was interested in protecting the settlers, and his calling out of rangers seems for this purpose. When Indians raids slackened in May, he disbanded Conner's company and the small county detachments. Webb suggested Houston may have formed the Johnson expedition to hold the rangers together, but the governor sent orders to discharge the units when it was clear they would not accomplish anything. He formed the company under Ross, as well as other units, to meet specific needs.

Authorization for six Mexican guides in some of the ranger commands has a sinister appeal to those who believe that Houston planned to set up a protectorate over part of Mexico, but the authorization was no more than an attempt to obtain men who were familiar with Indian territory. It does not seem likely that guides enlisted for service in north Texas would have much knowledge of the interior of Mexico. It has also been suggested that Houston's lack of significant effort to support Ford, hastening the discharge of the rangers in the valley, was in hopes that Cortina might have joined an expedition into Mexico, but this is excessively naive. Cortina might have been the worst sort of outlaw, but he was not a stupid outlaw. He used hatred of anything American as the cornerstone of his plans, and it was common knowledge in Texas that the failure of several of the revolutions in Mexico had been due largely to American support. The various factions in Mexico hated one another, but they hated the *gringos* more! Any invasion from Texas, however authorized or organized, would have met united resistance from all sections and classes in Mexico. Houston had to know this.

It is true he had earlier proposed a bill to establish a protectorate over Mexico while a U.S. Senator,[58] but he also strongly denounced any invasion of Mexico while he was governor, as mentioned earlier. The only unclear feature is what he had in mind in several letters he wrote to various people He may have made some sort of offer to Robert E. Lee, through a second party. Lee's reply is vague, although he declined whatever Houston was proposing.[59]

There was undoubtedly some attempt to raise money using English backers.[60] One such proposal was mentioned in Pike's recollections, at least indirectly, when he said he was approached after leaving the rangers by a man he knew only as "Captain Davis" who outlined a secret plan to invade Mexico and break away its northern states. Because of his position, Houston was not taking part, or so Davis told Pike. Always interested in a fight with a decent return, Pike turned down this offer because the proposed pay was only eighteen dollars a month and because there was little chance for success.[61]

On August 28, 1860, Houston wrote the most intriguing letter in this episode to his old companion, Ben McCulloch, to whom he hinted at "some work if it is undertaken....a mission of mercy and humanity....to elevate and exalt Mexico to a position among the nations of the world." He asked about manufacturing seven to ten-thousand rifles and described a special rifle he had designed. Probably weary with politics, he informed McCulloch he was definitely out of the race for the U.S. presidency. Then, at the last, he advised McCulloch never to marry![62]

This is the last reference to anything that might be considered a "plan" to invade Mexico.

In the closing months of 1860, Houston had too much on his mind to think about invasions. Frontier defense occupied much of his time; many of the documents in his papers have some bearing on Indian fighting. Seen in the context of the entire state, the Comanche raids involved few people, but they remained a danger threatening the expansion of the frontier. In the more populated eastern counties, where people were concerned with climate and crop prices and getting cotton to markets outside Texas, the Indian raids and Mexican bandits were remote and of no great interest. They worried instead about runaway slaves and the effects of the next national election, almost at hand in November.

Houston, with his broad view of his state and the nation, was well aware of all this, but the growing clamor over sectional rivalries, slavery and even the dissolution of the Union began to take more of his time even as he was still facing the Indian problem. At much the same time Houston was trying to form Ross' new company, he was also writing to a friend, expressing his personal views on secession: "There can be no aggravation of evil which would point to the dismemberment of the Union as its only panacea."[63] In this same letter he again mentioned he had abandoned any hope of being president and was joining a Union ticket to oppose Lincoln.

And, as always, Houston was faced with the nagging problem of paying the rangers. There can be little doubt most of the calls on the Secretary of War were to persuade the federal government to accept state troops and avoid the cost of frontier defense by Texas. It was a problem Houston had faced as President of Texas, it remained a problem for the early governors, and it would plague Texas' governors through the rest of the century. In his desperation, Houston even used money from the University Fund, which had been placed at his disposal by a special Act of the legislature,[64] creating some problems with other state officials.

Faced with continuing threats from the Comanches, Houston formed various ranger units in December 1860, as listed earlier. The company under Ross was the only ranger command from this time that distinguished itself. Barry did not post his twenty-four man unit into the field until January 10, 1861, and served only two months.[65] If Stockton formed his detachment, he left no written record; however, it is easy to see why Houston selected him after he had led a volunteer patrol in October and killed three Comanches north of Fort Chadbourne.[66] Dalrymple, barely out of service, was asked to come back and organize another company.[67]

In addition to the call on A.B. Burleson, already noted, the governor still felt the need for additional rangers. He called on E.W. Rogers, who had collected twenty or thirty men on a volunteer basis, and authorized him to bring the detachment to a full company and serve for three months. He was to join and serve with Ross. Houston issued his usual instructions about acquiring supplies by obtaining

Governor Sam Houston

bids and accepting the lowest offer. The rangers would have to use their own supplies until the state could assume this responsibility. Rogers was cautioned that any Indian south of the Red River would be considered hostile.[68]

Events were moving at a terrible, swift pace. The incidents and happenings of the past few decades had suddenly become an avalanche, and mere men, however powerful, could not resist the deluge. Indian raids and a few hundred rangers would be as nothing in a few months, overwhelmed by a national disaster on a scale men could not imagine.

Governor Houston issued a proclamation calling for an extra session of the legislature on December 17, 1860.[69] The following day, Sul Ross and his men would find the Comanches near the Pease River, unaware that their world was changing forever. Ten days later, Houston ordered the election of delegates to the Convention of Southern States.[70]

The split between the states, so dreaded by Houston, was drawing closer.

—9—

WAR AGAIN

T
exas began 1861 facing an unknown future. Abraham Lincoln had led the new Republican Party to victory in the national election and would become president in March. Just what this meant was uncertain, but most believed the election of Lincoln meant change in some manner. On the frontier, changes at the national level were a long distance away; the settlers continued to face the same old dangers much closer at hand.

The hero of the moment, the ranger captain L.S. "Sul" Ross, was back in Austin with his trophies on January 2, 1861. Governor Houston was already worrying about future Indian attacks, which were much more a certainty than changes in the nation's capital city, and instructed Thomas Harrison to form a seventy-man company and report to Belknap. The unit was in service almost immediately, with a muster-in date of January 10.[1]

Houston evidently wanted to keep a strong force in the Belknap area, since Ross' company would soon be discharged. He must have felt he was reciting an old story when he addressed the legislature on January 21, 1861, but this time there was an added threat.

> You have been convened in extra session, in view
> of the unsettled conditions of our national affairs,
> the continued invasion of our frontier by Indians, and
> the embarrassed condition of our Treasury.[2]

The governor continued, listing the ranger units called into service during 1860 and the efforts to pay them, including using the University Fund. Houston explained and ably defended his actions, rightly saying the alternative was abandoning the frontier settlements. Once again, he said the solution was the establishment of a permanent ranger regiment. In this connection, he made a prophetic comment.

> Should a contingency arise by which the Federal
> Army will be disbanded, and the Indians, now under
> treaty stipulations with the Federal Government, and
> controlled by them be turned loose, large appropria-
> tions will be necessary for the defense of our fron-
> tier.[3]

As usual, nothing came of his call for money. Houston was trying for, but not really expecting to obtain, financial support. He had already called up new units and designated William Dalrymple as commander, with the rank of colonel.[4]

Houston's fondness for personally controlling all military affairs caused trouble at this time. The popular hero Sul Ross appeared to be a new protege of the governor, and during his stay in Austin he may have received verbal instructions, perhaps even promises, from Houston. Even though he had no written authorization, Ross recruited some twenty new rangers and returned to his old base in Young County.[5]

Conditions had changed, and Captain Ross found he had to answer to Colonel Dalrymple, who had very definite ideas about the service. The new colonel even had a staff of four officers: two adjutants, a quartermaster, and an assistant quartermaster![6] Dalrymple took exception to the independent actions of the young captain, and an argument resulted. The issue seems petty now, but Ross had been accustomed to working alone and was probably as conscious of his position as Dalrymple was of his. Houston had caused the trouble by not sending Ross written orders.

Ross solved the misunderstanding by resigning. Houston refused to accept the resignation, cleared Ross of any blame, and forwarded new instructions on how to employ Ross and his new company.[7] Next, he wrote Ross, instructed him to form a new, enlarged company, and appointed him aide-de-camp with the rank of colonel.[8] Ross' acceptance would have completely snarled any effective control of the frontier units, but the young man refused any ranger service and Colonel Dalrymple remained in sole command of the frontier

units. He had a number of ranger companies to direct during this
time. While the resignation of Ross eliminated his company, most of
Ross' men remained in the area and joined other ranger commands.
Among the new companies was one led by the old ranger of the
Republic and sometime state senator, George B. Erath, who came to
duty March 8, 1861.[9]

In addition to the authorized ranger companies, a number of volunteer detachments were protecting their local areas. H.A. Hammer
had become a ranger captain in January 1860 and took an active part
in patrolling the Weatherford area in early 1861. Like many others, he
was also thinking of a possible dissolution of the Union. Hammer
wrote a friend attending the Secession Convention that he was considering a move against the federal garrison at Camp Cooper.[10] This
seems to be the earliest written suggestion of armed action in Texas,
although it is probable others on the frontier had the same thought.

The convention passed the Ordinance of Secession on February 1.
The state was not scheduled to vote on the measure until March 2,
but meanwhile Houston and the state legislature continued trying to
deal with frontier defense. It was as though the convention and the
legislature were in separate worlds, discussing completely unrelated
matters. In an attempt to provide additional troops, the legislature
passed an act allowing minute men volunteers to be paid while on
duty.[11] One group of men was planning the break up of the country,
the other was trying to defend the settlements.

Even while waiting to see how the vote on the Secession
Ordinance went, the convention made plans to seize the U.S. Army's
departmental headquarters in San Antonio. General David E. Twiggs,
the Department Commander, was a Southern sympathizer and did
not make even a token resistance; Ben McCulloch, now a colonel,
received his surrender. Twiggs not only surrendered the forces and
installations in San Antonio, he ordered all army forces and bases in
Texas to surrender! He was roundly castigated and removed from
command, but the damage was done.

No other army posts surrendered, but some Texans were now
openly considering forcing the issue. In Dallas, Richard Ward decided
to march on Camp Cooper and started the two-hundred mile trip
with sixteen volunteers! They furnished their horses, arms and equipment and headed west. Apparently the move was well advertised,

Main Plaza, San Antonio, 1861. This photograph shows Texas troops in the
Main Plaza, supposedly in connection with the surrender of General Twiggs.
This cannot be proven beyond a reasonable doubt-no Federal forces
are shown-but it is clearly from the general time frame and gives a faint and
fuzzy idea of the Texans of the late 1850s. *Courtesy of The Library of the
Daughters of the Republic of Texas, San Antonio.*

because twenty men in Lancaster wanted to go. Ward wrote them to
meet him in Weatherford, seventy miles west, and the two groups met
in that town, riding through a downpour.[12] Captain Hammer, who
had been the first to have the idea of capturing Camp Cooper, arrived
at Weatherford with only three men but then rode by Palo Pinto to
pick up another thirty volunteers before rejoining the column at
Belknap. The men at Belknap were joined by twenty-five additional
men under Captain A. Denton, and a "Mr. Faerier" arrived with additional reinforcements.

Official state troops—rangers—became part of the expedition.
Captain E. W. Rogers, who had met Ward in Waxahachie and encouraged his action, decided to become part of the movement and soon
started out on what passed for a road. Rogers sent word to other

ranger units on Elm Creek to join him. Captain Thomas L. Harrison was commanding a new ranger company which included many men from Ross' disbanded command. Another ranger unit led by David L. Sublett stopped patrolling and joined near Camp Cooper.[13]

Colonel Dalrymple, nominally in command of these ranger companies, rode in and assumed control of the various official and volunteer companies and detachments. Ward, however, continued to be a major individual player in the developing action. By coincidence, Middleton Johnson and his wife happened to be visiting in the area, staying at the army post and a nearby ranch. The one-time colonel was soon pressed into service as a courier between Dalrymple and Captain S.D. Carpenter, 1st Infantry, the post commander. Ward was careful to mention that Johnson had no command responsibility.

The state forces camped near the post for three days. The combined ranger/volunteer command heavily outnumbered Carpenter's garrison, and finally he sent a letter on February 18 asking what the Texans planned, as he could only infer they were contemplating some hostile move. Dalrymple replied they had the objective of reducing Camp Cooper. In case this was not clear, he followed with a terse note later in the day demanding the surrender of the garrison, supplies, arms and equipment.[14] The two sides carried on a gentlemanly and refined dialogue for the next two days. Carpenter was in a hopeless position; even if he was able to fight his way out of the camp, he was still in the midst of nowhere facing hopeless odds. The Texans had no wish to shed blood. Captain Carpenter surrendered Camp Cooper on February 20 and marched out the next day.

The federal infantrymen left Camp Cooper, marching down one side of Clear Fork, and the Texans entered by the opposite bank, avoiding any meeting between enemies who had been friends only a few days earlier. Dalrymple immediately stationed Rogers' company in the abandoned post and established his headquarters there. The rangers were in possession by about eleven in the morning. Ward said they gave three cheers for the Lone Star, after which the volunteers scattered to their homes.

It had all seemed very easy—probably the way they envisioned the separation of the states. The rangers had unknowingly taken part in one of the earliest forced takeovers of U.S. Army posts, but it was just part of their daily work. Their main task was frontier protection, and Dalrymple stayed in Cooper just long enough to organize his new command. On February 24 he left with Harrison's and part of Mays' and Sublett's companies, in all slightly over a hundred men.[15] They took pack animals, with forage to last a month. The expedition was much the same as a hundred earlier scouts; some of Harrison's rangers killed two Indians a few days out, but that was the last word from the expedition heard by the rangers remaining in Camp Cooper.[16]

National events were moving at crash speed, and even in Texas conditions were changing daily. The convention had taken over control of Texas to a large degree, and on February 27, three days after the rangers left Cooper on their extended scout, it divided the frontier into three zones: Rip Ford was in command of the Rio Grande line; Ben McCulloch had the line midway between Fort McIntosh and Fort Duncan, north to Fort Chadbourne; his brother Henry was in charge of the frontier from Chadbourne to the Red River. The choices for the new commanders were sound; the men were experienced and were probably the best choices that could have been made. The three men assumed their new rank of colonel and began forming their commands.

Little or no attention was paid to what actions the state legislature had taken in recent weeks. Henry McCulloch had been given the same rank and the same region to defend as Dalrymple, and if the convention had any idea there were ranger units near Cooper, the knowledge was not revealed in any orders given McCulloch. He started north from Austin, moving to Brown County and organizing five mounted companies on the way. Joined by at least two-hundred civilians, the column advanced on Camp Colorado seemingly unaware of what had happened at Camp Cooper. McCulloch received the surrender of the army post and went on to Fort Chadbourne, taking command of that installation as well. While there, he met the troops that had just surrendered to the rangers and volunteers at Cooper. Taking his position seriously, McCulloch demanded the federals surrender again because their capture by the rangers had not been authorized by the convention! This was done; the disgusted soldiers were willing to do anything to halt what was now a farce and leave.

Colonel Henry McCulloch was not quite finished. Leaving garrisons in Colorado and Chadbourne, he marched to Camp Cooper and demanded the surrender of Captain Rogers and his ranger company! Poor Rogers must have wondered who was in charge, but he dutifully gave up the post. He did report all this to Governor Houston.[17] Rogers' mission, as he saw it, was fighting Indians, and McCulloch could have the post and welcome. As he told the *Dallas Herald* in a letter written March 10, "I have surrendered the Post and property to him—all anxious for a change and a chase or hunt for the savage foe. Expect to start on the 17th inst. for headwaters of the Colorado River."

When Dalrymple returned from his scout and learned what had happened, he bowed to the will of the convention. McCulloch recommended the two commands be consolidated.[18] McCulloch was placed in charge, and the ranger and his staff remained on duty until June 22, probably trying to stay out of the way.[19]

At the end of yet another chapter in ranger history, the ranger commands' periods of service expired and they were disbanded or consolidated with other state forces. Ewen Cameron's company near Fredericksburg was mustered out on April 10. Sublett left May 14; Harrison's company was discharged June 22. Erath and A.B. Burleson were exceptions and remained in service until December 1861.[20]

By that time, Fort Sumter had been shelled and taken and a real war was in the making. Old Sam Houston had refused to accept what was at hand and was no longer the governor of Texas, which had voted to join the new Confederacy, although not without many dissenting votes and voices. Generally, the frontier counties were in favor of continuing in the Union, but they acquiesced to the majority. Life for them did not change much; whether governed from Richmond or Washington, theirs was still a harsh life—Hell on horses and women and with the ever-present threat of Indians.

Confederate Texas did the best it could for the next four years as demands for military service in distant areas drained away forces formed for frontier protection. Patterned on the dream of a ranger regiment, the troops remaining in Texas to guard its frontiers did not earn the reputation or possess the fire of the earlier units, and it would be 1870 before ranger companies again defended the frontiers of Texas.

But that is another part of the story....

ENDNOTES

CHAPTER ONE

ROADS WEST

1. See Frederick Wilkins, *The Highly Irregular Irregulars, Texas Rangers in the Mexican War* (Austin: Eakin Press, 1990), for the story of the Texas Volunteer Rangers in the Mexican War.

2. Frederick Wilkins, *The Legend Begins: The Texas Rangers 1823-1845* (Austin, Tex: State House Press, 1996) has an updated account of Hays' service during the Republic of Texas era.

3. El Paso del Norte was not the contemporary El Paso, Texas, but the Mexican city now known as Juarez.

4. *Samuel Maverick: Texas 1803-1870*, ed. Rena Maverick Green (San Antonio: Privately printed, 1952), 333-42.

5. Henry W. Barton, *Texas Volunteers in the Mexican War* (Wichita Falls, Tex.: Texian Press, 1970), 117.

6. Ibid., 105.

7. James K. Greer, *Colonel Jack Hays* (New York: E.P. Dutton & Co., Inc., 1952), 217-26 retraces the route. John Caperton, *Sketch of Colonel John C. Hays, Texas Ranger* (typed manuscript, The Center for American History, University of Texas at Austin) has an eye witness version. The narrative described here is based on Caperton and Maverick's recollections and Greer's modern reconstruction.

8. Caperton stated this took place later, after they were well down into the Big Bend, but it seems likely it occurred well before.

9. The Comanche War Trail was a path Comanche raiders had used for generations on their way south into Mexico. By the mid 1840s it had been beaten into a broad roadway, crossing the Pecos at what later became known as Horsehead Crossing. It went generally south from present day Fort Stockton, following the natural gaps through the broken country to Marathon. Continuing south, the trail kept east of the Santiago Mountains, cutting through the only pass through the southern end of the mountains and onto the more level country north of the Chisos Mountains. The trail divided in this region, one branch continuing south, the other going southwest to the San Carlos Crossing on the Rio Grande and across into Mexico. Army maps of the

1880s clearly traced the War Trail, the only man-made road in the area. Modern paved roads going south from Fort Stockton into the Big Bend follow much the same route.

10. The restored ruins of Leaton's "fort" are now a state park just east of *i* present day Presidio.

11. Barton, 117.

12. Caperton complained they never received proper credit for opening the way west through Texas. He claimed the government afterwards sent parties that followed their trial and laid out roads and established army posts along their old route.

13. Kenneth F. Neighbours, "The Report of the Expedition of Major Robert S. Neighbors to El Paso in 1849," *Southwestern Historical Quarterly,* Vol. 60, No. 4 (April 1957), 528-32. Hereafter *SHQ*.

14. John Salmon Ford left a huge body of material, his recollections plus much additional material, newspaper clippings, Army orders, reports, etc. His approximately 1,200 handwritten pages are available in a six-volume type-script, available in the Center for American History at the University of Texas at Austin and in the Texas State Library. Material from this source will be referred to as Ford, *Memoirs*. In recent years, Stephen B. Oates edited this work and it was published as *Rip Ford's Texas* (Austin: University of Texas Press, 1987). Because the book is more readily available, wherever possible it has been used as a source for Ford's actions and will be cited as Ford, *Texas*.

15. Neighbours, "Expedition," 529. This section is based on his report and the more detailed account in Ford, *Texas*, 113-29.

16. Ford, *Texas*, 128. The Spanish established the Mission San Saba on the San Saba River in the mid Eighteenth Century. Comanche attacks destroyed the mission proper but left the stone presidio in good shape. It was rediscovered by ranger expeditions in the 1840s. The Horsehead Crossing was named by later white explorers, the name coming from the large numbers of horse skeletons mired in the treacherous banks.

17. Neighbours, "Expedition," 528.

18. Ford, *Texas*, 128.

19. See A. B. Bender, "Opening Routes Across West Texas," *SHQ*, Vol. 37, No. 2 (October 1933), 121-22 for details of this expedition.

20. Neighbours, "Expedition," 532.

CHAPTER TWO
THE RANGERS AND THE U.S. ARMY

1. *Texas State Gazette*, December 29, 1849.
2. Ibid., October 27, 1849.
3. Brooke to Maj Gen Jones, August 31, 1849. Texas State Library, 31st

Cong., 1st Sess., House Executive Doc. No. 5, 143.

4. Ibid., 138-39.

5. Ibid., 141.

6. R. E. Sutton to Governor H. Bell, January 1, 1850, Texas State Library, Governor's Letters, hereafter GL.

7. *Texas State Gazette*, August 25, 1849.

8. Ford, *Texas*, 141-42.

9. Ibid., 143.

10. Ibid., 143-45.

11. Ford, *Memoirs*, Vol. 3, 600.

12. Ford, *Texas*, 147. This is undoubtedly the same man as the Captain Gamble mentioned in the *Texas State Gazette*.

13. Winfrey H. Dorman and James M. Day, editors, *The Indian Papers of Texas and the Southwest 1825-1916*, Vol. 3, 113. Hereafter Indian Papers.

14. Ford, *Memoirs*, Vol. 3, 601.

15. Ford, *Texas*, 151.

16. Ibid., 151-54.

17. *Texas State Gazette*, March 2 and March 9, 1850.

18. Order No. 11, Headquarters 8th Department, San Antonio, March 6, 1850, in Ranger Papers-Correspondence, 1854-1861. Hereafter RP-C.

19. J. W. Wilbarger, *Indian Depredations in Texas*, 1889. Reprint (Austin: State House Press, 1985), 666-71.

20. GL. Brooke to Governor Bell, August 10, 1850. Wallace did continue in service, forming a new company at Fort Inge on March 23, 1851. A muster roll in the Military Reference Branch, National Archives, shows it as "Capt. William A.A. Wallace company of Texas Mounted Volunteers, called into service by Maj. General M. Brooke." The seventy-seven man unit was on duty until early May 1851.

21. Henry E. McCulloch, Texas Mounted Volunteers, November 5, 1850-May 5, 1851, (Fort Murrill), Ranger Papers-Muster and Pay Rolls, 1846-1861. Hereafter RP-Rolls

22. Ford, *Texas*, 147.

23. Wilbarger, 612.

24. GL. Henry McCulloch to Major George Deas, January 6, 1851.

25. RP-Rolls. Henry McCulloch, Texas Mounted Volunteers, May 5-November 4, 1851, (Ft. Martin Scott.)

26. Wilbarger, 613.

27. GL, Bvt Col H. Wilson to Bvt Major George Deas, November 24, 1849. The seemingly strange location of some army dispatches in the governor's office is because the cooperative Department Commander furnished the governor with copies of any correspondence relating to the state troops.

28. GL. P.W. Humphrey to Major Deas, December 1, 1849.

29. GL. Brooke to Bell, December 23, 1949.

30. *Indian Papers*, Vol. 3, 110.

31. Ibid., 114-19.

32. Ibid., Brooke to Scott, May 28, 1850, 119-21.

33. Ibid., Bell to Brooke, June 4, 1850, 121-23.

34. Ford, *Texas*, 154.

35. This narrative is based on Ford, *Texas*, 154-62. The commendation is quoted in full on page 162.

36. Ford, *Texas*, 170-73.

37. Ibid., 162-64.

38. Ford, *Memoirs*, Vol. 3, 601.

39. Ford, *Texas*, 173.

40. Ibid., 174-78.

41. Ford has an account of this fight in *Texas*, 177-80. Wilbarger, 616-20, also has a version which agrees with Ford in most details. However, he has the fight's taking place in December 1850.

42. Ford, *Memoirs*, Vol. 3, 601.

43. Ford, *Texas*, 185-86.

44. Ibid., 186-87.

45. GL. John H. Rollins to Governor Bell, October 30, 1850.

46. GL. M. Duval to Governor Bell, October 20, 1850.

47. GL. Brooke to Bell, November 12, 1850.

48. GL. Brooke to Bell, February 7, 1851.

49. Ford, *Texas*, 188.

50. *San Antonio Ledger* as reprinted in the *Texas State Gazette*, October 11, 1851, quoted by Ford, *Texas*, 189.

CHAPTER THREE

THE RANGERS AS STATE TROOPS

1. Ford, *Texas*, 196.

2. For a complete account of Carvajal, see Ernest C. Shearer, "The Carvajal Disturbances," *SHQ*, Vol.55, No. 2 (October 1951), 201-30. A contemporary account is in Emanuel Domenech, *Missionary Adventures in Texas and Mexico* (London: Longman, Brown, Green, Longmans and Roberts, 1858), 347.

3. Ford, *Texas*, 196-97.

4. Ibid., 205.

5. Domenech, 176.

6. Ibid., 228.

7. These actions are outlined in a report the adjutant general made to the governor. GL, Gillett to Governor Bell, October 10, 1852.

8. GL. C.M. Conrad to Governor Bell, September 30, 1852.

9. GL. Gillett to Governor Bell, October 10, 1852.

10. GL. Shaw to Governor Bell, September 22, 1852.

11. GL. Davis to Governor Bell, December 12, 1852.

12. RP-Rolls. Owen Shaw, Texas Mounted Volunteers, August 18, 1852-February 17, 1853; G.K. Lewis, Texas Mounted Volunteers, September 14, 1852-March 13, 1853.

13. *Indian Papers*, Vol. 3, 184-85, Pease to the citizens of Burnet, Bell, McLennan and Williamson counties and to the citizens of Bosque county, May 8, 1854.

14. RP-C. Letter from J. P. Taylor, Office Commissary General Subsistence to the Adjutant General, January 17, 1859.

15. RP-C. Pease to James W. Throckmorton, February 5, 1856. Special agents finally paid the former rangers during March and April 1856. The files contain a number of letters from Governor Pease to the several agents, instructing them to settle with the companies. Texas was reimbursed for these expenses by an Act of Congress approved March 3, 1855. Treasury Department, J. D. Fuller to Col. S. Cooper, A. G. USA, Jan 8, 1859.

16. RP-C. Contract between Captain Giles S. Boggess and Doctor A. J. Miller, December 1, 1854.

17. The companies in the files are: Giles S. Boggess, Company A (San Antonio), John G. Walker, Company B; Wm. R. Henry, Company C; William Fitzhugh, Company D; Patrick H. Rogers, Company F.

18. This was on December 2, 1854.

19. Ranger Papers-Quarter Master Records, November 1, 1854. Hereafter RP-QM.

20. San Antonio *Zeitung*, December 11, 1854. Quoted in Frederick L. Olmstead, *A Journey through Texas*. 1857. Reprint (Austin: University of Texas Press, 1989), 507.

21. RP-Rolls. William R. Henry. Texas Mounted Volunteers (San Antonio) December 14, 1854-March 31, 1855.

22. *Texas State Gazette*, March 10, 1855.

CHAPTER FOUR

CALLAHAN'S RAID

1. See *Indian Papers*, Vol. 3, 222-23, for sample letters.

2. *Indian Papers*, Vol. 3, 224-28. Petition of Citizens of Bexar County to E.M. Pease, July 12, 1855.

3. A. J. Sowell, *Early Settlers and Indian Fighters of Southwest Texas*. 1900. Reprinted as *Texas Indian Fighters* (Austin: State House Press, 1986), 429.

4. GL. Pease to Smith, June 20, 1855.

5. GL. Pease to James H. Callahan, July 5, 1855.

6. A brief summary of Callahan's service is in Ernest C. Shearer, "The Callahan Expedition, 1855," *SHQ*, Vol. 54, No. 4 (April 1951), 430-31. His ranger service is treated more fully in Wilkins, *The Legend Begins*, 116, 119.

7. RP-Rolls. Captain James H. Callahan, Texas Rangers\Mounted Rangers (Rio Blanco.) July 20-October 19, 1855.

8. GL. Pease to Callahan, July 25, 1855.

9. *Indian Papers*, Vol. 3, 228. E. M. Pease to Citizens of Bexar County, July 25, 1855.

10. RP-C. Order No. 1, 1st Lt E Burleson, August 1, August 3, 1855.

11. RP-QM. Burleson turned in vouchers for both trips January 8, 1856.

12. Ibid. Voucher and receipts signed by Clark Ridley, January 19, 1856.

13. RP-QM 1855. At least three different smiths did work for the company, according to various vouchers submitted for payment.

14. *Indian Papers*, Vol. 3, 240-43. Jones to Pease, September 22, 1855.

15. Ibid., 230-31. Newspaper Item Concerning Indian Depredations (August 6, 1855).

16. GL W.R. Henry to Governor Pease, September 2, 1855.

17. GL. Pease to BG P. S. Smith, September 5, 1855.

18. GL. Pease to C. Evans, Ben E. Edwards & H. B. Saunders, September 5, 1855.

19. *Texas State Gazette*, September 22, 1855.

20. P.F. Smith to S. Cooper, September 8, 1855. Quoted in Shearer, "Callahan Expedition," 436.

21. RP-C. Callahan to Burleson, Sept 12, 1855.

22. *Plum Creek Almanac*, Vol. 3, No. 2. The Caldwell Historical Society reprinted notes made by J.S. McDowell, a member of Callahan's expedition. These notes were given to John Ford many years later, and Ford used them to compile an account of the Callahan raid, as part of his life of Ed Burleson. They were reprinted in the *San Antonio News*, January 6, 1893. Hereafter referred to as McDowell.

23. Sowell, 530-34.

24. McDowell. The following narrative, except as noted, is based on his account. Although he is generally accurate, his time frame for these events in late September/early October may be in error by one or two days.

25. Callahan to Pease, October 13, 1855. This letter was printed in the *Texas State Gazette*, October 20, 1855, and is quoted in Shearer, "Callahan Expedition," 437.

26. Sowell, 527-28.

27. RP-C. Captain S. Burbank to Assnt. Adjt. General, Department of Texas, San Antonio, October 4, 1855.

28. GL. Governor Pease to Lt. Ed Burleson, October 4, 1855.

29. This is known only by a reference in the letter Pease sent Callahan on

October 10.

30. This was Jesse Sumpter, quoted in Shearer, "Callahan Expedition," 442.

31. RP-C. Capt. S. Burbank to Assnt. Adjt. General, Department of Texas, October 8, 1855.

32. GL. Pease to Callahan, October 10, 1855.

33. GL. Pease to Smith, October 13, 1855.

34. Ford and Henry McCulloch were among other well known citizens in San Antonio at this time, awaiting intelligence and reinforcements before joining Callahan, *Galveston Daily News*, January 8, 1893.

35. RP-C. BG P.F. Smith to Lt. Col. L. Thomas, Assnt. A.G., Headquarters of the Army, October 17, 1855.

36. GL. Pease to Pitts, October 18, 1855.

37. RP-Rolls. James H. Callahan, as cited. Nathaniel Benton, Texas Rangers\Mounted Rangers\Mounted Volunteers (Leona River), September 15-October 15, 1855; William R. Henry, September 15-October 15, 1855.

38. GL. Pease to Smith, October 17, 1855.

39. GL. Governor Pease to the Gentlemen of the Senate and House of Representatives, November 22, 1855.

40. GL. Pease to Pitts, December 18, 1855.

41. RP-C. The affidavits are too numerous to cite, comprising a large part of the papers for 1856 and into 1857.

42. Shearer, "Callahan Expedition," 446-50, covers this part of the Callahan story in some detail, It is interesting to note the final settlement of the claims took place in 1876! Captain Cuchanan is probably Captain Burbank.

43. Olmstead, 333.

44. The *Texas State Gazette* and the *Bastrop Advertiser* were active in this endeavor.

45. Ford, *Texas*, 214-15.

46. Ibid.

47. Callahan to Pease, October 13, 1855, reprinted in the *Texas State Gazette*, October 20, 1855.

48. *San Antonio Herald*, October 16, 1855.

49. Olmstead, 507.

CHAPTER FIVE

NEW YEAR—OLD PROBLEMS

1. RP-Rolls. William Tom, Texas Volunteers (San Antonio) October 18, 1855; William G. Tobin, Mounted Texas Rangers\Volunteers (San Antonio) October 12-November 15, 1855; Levi English, Mounted Men\Rangers, August 6-November 13, 1855. RP-C, Pease to Gentlemen of Senate and House of Representatives, January 3, 1856.

2. RP-Rolls. John W. Sansom, Texas Mounted Rangers\Volunteers (Middle Town, Comal County) for protection of upper Blanco's Curey's upper Guadalupe and Pedernales settlements, April 16-July 16, 1856; John M. Davenport, Mounted Volunteers Minute Men (Sabinal settlements) March 13, 1856-June 1, 1857. RP-C, Pease to Gentlemen of Senate and House of Representatives, August 4, 1856.

3. RP-Rolls. Captain John M. Davenport.

4. RP-C. December 7, December 19 and December 19, 1857, to officers as noted.

5. GL. Pease to the Lieutenant selected to command the company of mounted men enrolled by Thomas C. Frost, December 7, 1857.

6. GL. To Your Excellency, E. M. Pease from John H. Conner, December 11th 1857.

7. H.R. Runnels was the new governor.

8. RP-C. Lieutenant Thomas C. Frost to H.R. Runnels, January 8, 1858. The Neighbors mentioned by Frost was Major Robert Simpson Neighbors, who had commanded the 1848 expedition described in Chapter One to locate a road to El Paso. At this time, 1858, he was Supervising Indian Agent of Texas. Neighbors was in charge of the Indians in the two agencies in Texas, the Comanche and the Brazos agencies. He fiercely defended his Indians from what he considered false charges that they sometimes raided nearby farms and settlements. Ford generally stood with Neighbors in wanting to give the agency Indians every opportunity to adjust to settled life. (Ford, *Texas*, 219-20), but most settlers along the frontier did not share this view.

9. RP-C. John S. Hodges to Runnels, January 9, 1858.

10. RP-Rolls.

11. Allen Lee Hamilton, *Sentinel of the Southern Plains* (Fort Worth: Texas Christian University Press, 1988), 65-95, has an interesting modern account of this incident. He clearly shows the contemporary opinion outside Texas, as late as the mid 1870s, of what was considered the highly magnified Indian danger in Texas.

12. Olmstead, 160. Like most contemporary writers and observers, Olmstead made no distinction between Mexican nationals and Texans of Mexican ancestry.

13. GL. John Withers, Asst. Adjt. General to E. M. Pease, October 14, 1857.

14. RP-Rolls. Captain G. H. Nelson, Texas Mounted Militia, October 10, 1857-December 28, 1857.

15. GL. Nelson to Pease, November 28, 1857.

16. GL. Nelson to Pease, December 17, 1857.

CHAPTER SIX
SENIOR CAPTAIN "RIP" FORD

1. "Memoirs of George Bernard Erath," *SHQ*, Vol. 27, No. 2 (October 1923), 150-51.
2. *Indian Papers*, Vol. 3, 265-66. Pease to Guy M. Bryan & John H. Regan, November 3, 1857.
3. Ibid., 269-70. Congressional Message, Gentlemen of the Senate and House of Representatives, December 22, 1857.
4. Ibid., 270-71. H.R. Runnels to the President of the Senate, January 22, 1858.
5. *Texas State Gazette*, January 30, 1858, quoted in Ford, *Texas*, 223.
6. Erath, 151.
7. GL. To all whom these presents shall come: Executive Mansion, Austin, Texas, January 28, 1858. Ford received his nickname in the Mexican War, during which he served as Hays' adjutant during the campaign in Central Mexico. Besides fighting, he was responsible for keeping unit records, including making the necessary notations on individual service records. A family story said he marked "Rest in Peace, Ford" on the service record of any Texans killed in the campaign. Often in a hurry, he shortened this to "RIP, Ford," a name that stayed with him the rest of his life.
8. GL. Runnels to Ford, January 28, 1858.
9. *Texas State Gazette*, January 30, 1858, quoted in Ford, *Texas*, 223.
10. RP-Rolls. John S. Ford, February 5, 1858.
11. RP-C. General Order No. 2, February 8, 1858. John S. Ford, Capt. Commdg Texas Frontier.
12. Ibid., Ford to S. Swenson, February 10, 1858.
13. Ibid., Ford to Runnels, February 13, 1858.
14. This unit should not be confused with the company led by G.H. Nelson in the so-called Cart War.
15. Ford, *Texas*, 225. Ford had discretion about retaining units in service. He had decided to disband Connor's company before he left Austin. He evidently had strong reservations about Frost's command. Fearing he might have been hasty, he later obtained an appointment for Frost as a lieutenant colonel in Henry McCulloch's regiment early in the Civil War.
16. *Indian Papers*, Vol. 3, 275-76. Ford to Runnels, March 11, 1858.
17. Ford, *Texas*, p 225.
18. As cited in note 16.
19. *Indian Papers*, Vol. 3, 277-79. Ford to Runnels, March 31, 1858.
20. These individual reports are reprinted in Indian Papers, Vol 3, 277-79.
21. Ibid., 281-82, T.S. Anderson to Ford, April 8, 1858.
22. Ibid., 282, C. Cowan to T.S. Anderson, May 2, 1858.

23. Ibid., 283, H.R. Runnels to J. Williams, May 5, 1858.

24. Ibid., John H. Connor to H.R. Runnels, May 5, 1858.

25. Ford, *Texas*, 227.

26. In later years, Ford wrote a tribute to Ross giving him credit for much of the success of the expedition. It is one of many papers in his *Memoirs*, and is reprinted on 439-56 of Ford, *Texas*.

27. Ford, *Texas*, 228.

28. Ibid., 229.

29. Ibid., 237.

30. Ibid., 229.

31. Ibid.

32. GL. John S. Ford to H.R. Runnels, May 22, 1858. This is Ford's unedited account and indicates he was still under pressure. The version used in this book is the typed copy in the State Archives. It is presumably an exact copy of the original, with some added [*sic*] by the typist. Other misspelled words are not noted. There are some minor variations in the Indian names from those used in Ford, *Texas*, 231.

33. The word blotted out could have the degree of the wound, or uncertainty over the spelling of the ranger's name. Paschal's name has been added in parenthesis.

34. *Indian Papers*, Vol. 3, 286. Runnels to Ford, May 28, 1858.

35. Ibid., 287, Address by H.R. Runnels to Captain Ford's Company of Texas Rangers, May 28, 1858.

36. Ford, *Texas*, 234 - 235.

37. In *Texas,* 237, Ford quoted an Indian captain who said sixty prisoners were divided among the agency Indians. Ford's report mentions eighteen.

38. *Indian Papers*, Vol. 3, 289-90. Ford to H.R. Runnels, June 3, 1858.

39. Ibid., 290-91. J. Williams to H.R. Runnels, June 24, 1858.

40. Ford, *Texas*, 241. RP-Rolls, Lt. William N.P. Marlin, February 24-August 24, 1858, July 15-November 15, 1858.

41. RP-Rolls. James Bourland, Mounted Volunteers, October 28, 1858-January 28, 1859.

42. Ibid., John S. Ford, Texas Rangers (Austin), February 5, 1858-August 5, 1858.

43. GL. Runnels to Ford, November 2, 1858.

44. GL. Proclamation signed by Runnels, November 10, 1858.

45. RP-C. Contract between John S. Ford and S.M. Swenson, August 3, 1858. Copy in Comptroller's Office, dated May 8, 1861.

46. RP-Rolls. John S. Ford, November 10, 1858-May 10, 1859.

47. *Texas State Gazette*, November 27, 1858.

48. Olmstead, 287. This is just one example. Olmstead and his brother could afford and bought the best weapons available, and they apparently believed

Texans did likewise.

49. Ford, *Texas*, 242-43.

50. *Dallas Herald*, quoting Van Dorn's report.

51. Ford, *Texas*, 243-46.

52. Ibid., 247.

53. Ibid., 247-48.

54. Ibid., 249-59.

55. Documentation on this incident is in U.S. Senate Executive Documents, 36th Congress, 1st session, Vol. I, Document No. 2, 588-604. The *Texas State Gazette* printed letters by Ford and E.J. Gurley from April 30 through May 21, 1858.

56. RP-Rolls. Williams was given another unit on November 2, 1858, remaining on duty until August 16, 1859.

57. RP-C. John Williams to Runnels, October 25, 1858.

58. Ibid., Hillary Ryan to Runnels, October 30, 1858.

59. Ibid., Runnels to Bourland, October 4, 1858, October 6, 1858.

60. RP-Rolls. James Bourland, as cited.

61. Ford, *Texas*, 239-40.

62. Erath, 151-53.

63. GL. Runnels to Allison Nelson & Other Citizens of the Frontier, June 6, 1859.

64. GL. Runnels, Instructions to Messrs Erath, Coke, Smith, Brown and Steiner, June 6, 1859.

65. Erath, 153.

66. Ibid., 154. RP-Rolls, John Henry Brown, Texas Mounted Rangers (Two Detachments) June 28-September 12, 1859.

67. GL. Capt. John Henry Brown to Major B.G. Neighbors, July 14, 1859.

68. John Henry Brown, *History of Texas*, Vol. 2 (St Louis: L.E. Daniel, 1893), 378.

69. GL. Runnels to Brown, August 4, 1859.

70. A complete account of the expulsion of the agency Indians is in Kenneth F. Neighbours, "Indian Exodus Out of Texas in 1859," *West Texas Historical Association Year Book*, Vol. 36, 80-97. The details, other than Brown's involvement, are not part of the ranger story.

71. GL. Brown to Thomas, August 6, 1859. Thomas to Brown, August 8, 1859.

72. GL. Brown to Runnels, August 19, 1859.

73. RP-Rolls, as cited above for Brown.

74. Brown, *History of Texas*, Vol. 2, 279. There may be more to this tale. Walter Prescott Webb, *The Texas Rangers* (Boston-New York: Houghton Mifflin Company, 1935), 172, has an undocumented story that a man named Ed Cornett shot Neighbors. An ex-ranger named France Peveler said he was

one of the ranger party who found Cornett and handled him without benefit—
or hindrance—of the law.

CHAPTER SEVEN
THE CORTINA PROBLEM

1. This section is based on Ford, *Texas,* 260-63; W.H. Chatfield, *Twin Cities
of the Border* (New Orleans: E.P. Brandao, 1893), 14; and Juan Cortina, "Juan
Cortina and the Texas-Mexico Frontier 1859-1877", Jerry D. Thompson, ed.,
Southwestern Studies No.9 (El Paso: Texas Western Press, 1994), Introduction,
1-2.
  2. Chatfield, 15.
  3. RP-C. Runnels to W.G. Tobin, October 13, 1859.
  4. RP-Rolls. Capt. William G. Tobin's Company of Mounted Texas
Rangers, 12 October, 1855.
  5. Ibid., Captain William G. Tobin's Company of Texas Volunteers from the
eighteenth day of October 1859 to the third day of November 1859.
  6. GL. Stephen Powers to Governor Runnels, October 23, 1859.
  7. Based on a later report by Major Samuel Peter Heintzelman, who would
soon report as military commander of the Brownsville district. Tobin's company arrived in Brownsville the night of November 10, 1859, after a two-week
march from San Antonio. He mentions this in a report to the governor, which
also confirms the accidental death of Jackson. Texas State Library, Record
Group 301, *Correspondence Files of Governor Sam Houston,* Tobin to
Runnels, November 16, 1859. Hereafter *Houston Correspondence.*
  8. RP-C. P.Jordan to Dr. W., November 14, 1859.
  9. RP-Rolls. Tobin's muster roll, October 18, 1859.
  10. Ibid., Muster Roll of Captain John Littleton's Company of Texas
Rangers, 15th Day of October, 1859-Jan 14, 1860. The title of this roll is
somewhat misleading, as it is the roll of Tobin's old company including men
and events until the unit was discharged in 1860.
  11. *Houston Correspondence.* Tobin to Runnels, November 27, 1859. In this
report. Tobin lists the four rangers killed on November 21, 1859. The four men
are listed on company muster rolls as killed on that date. However, Tobin mentions Nicholas R. Milett, who is carried on the roll as Nicholas R. Mallett.
  12. RP-Rolls, Muster Roll of Captain John Littleton's Company of Texas
Rangers, 15th Day of October, 1859-Jan 14, 1860.
  13. Ibid., Captain Henry W. Berry, November 10, 1859-December 20, 1859.
  14. As Heintzelman was not a witness to the action, it is difficult to see how
he made the observation. He had been designated army commander of a considerable force and sent south to end the Cortina trouble. During the march to
Brownsville the danger from Cortina seemed to lessen, and when Heintzelman

finally arrived in Brownsville on December 6, 1859, he was accompanied by a company of the 2nd Cavalry and units of the 3rd Artillery. Samuel P. Heintzelman maintained a journal during this period, edited by Jerry Thompson and published as *Fifty Miles and a Fight: Major Samuel Heintzelman's Journal of Texas and the Cortina War* (Austin: Texas State Historical Association, 1998). Tobin's version of Santa Rita is contained in his report to Runnels on November 27, cited above. According to him, his mixed force rode to within a half mile of the main Cortina camp. The officers had a conference, decided it would be foolish to attack a fortified position and decided to return to Brownsville, gather reinforcements and plan another attack.

15. Printed in "Difficulties on the Southwestern Frontier," House Executive Document No. 52, 36th Congress, 1st Session, Serial No. 1050, 79-82.

16. GL. Tobin to Runnels, December 16, 1859.

17. RP-Rolls. Captain Henry W. Berry.

18. Tobin, as cited in #16 above. Peter Tumlinson and thirty-nine men from Atasocsa County had joined Tobin on November 22. Other detachments came and went, but Tumlinson's company and another company commanded by Captain G.J. Hampton were officially mustered into state service. In his journal, Heintzelman has a considerably different version of what came to be known as the fight at El Ebonal. (Heintzelman, *Fifty Miles,* 138-41) He does not mention Stoneman and his cavalry company. The three ranger units mustered about 125 men between them, and the major had little good to say about any of them. He noted at one point that neither the army nor the Texans could move through the dense chaparral. In another disparaging remark, Heintzelman noted that he easily passed the rangers, struggling in the brush, while he stayed on the road! He complained they could easily have captured the enemy cannon and concluded that he would have been better off without the rangers.

19. House Executive Document, No. 81, 36th Congress, 1st Session, Serial No. 1056, 8, printed as part of "Troubles in Texas." Heintzelman's Report to Bvt. Col. Robert E. Lee, March 1, 1860, does not always coincide with ranger reports or recollections.

20. Ford, *Texas*, 265-66.

21. RP-C. Runnels to Ford and Highsmith, November 17, 1859.

22. RP-Rolls. Lt. Joseph Walker, Texas Rangers\Mounted Volunteers. Banquete Texas, Nov 30, 59-Jan 20, 60.

23. Ford, *Texas*, 266-67.

24. GL. Ford to Runnels, December 16, 1859.

25. Ford, *Texas*, 268-69.

26. RP-C. Contract between John S. Ford, Major State Troops, and W.G. Woodhouse, December 20, 1859. At this time, many rangers were using the Sharps breech loading carbine or rifle. These weapons fired a paper cartridge,

and obtaining these cartridges was not always an easy matter. Later, one man in Ford's company had a full time job making paper cartridges for the unit.

27. Ford, *Texas*, 269-70. Ford identifies Herron as Captain "Harmon."

28. Ibid.,270-75.

29. RP-Rolls. RP-C, List of wounded in the battle of Rio Grande City Dec 27th 1859. Recd, Jany 9, 1860.

30. "Difficulties on the Southwestern Frontier," 97-98.

31. "Troubles in Texas," 2-14. Heintzelman's journal has very little on this fight. He indicates the army's soldiers were following Ford and the rangers. At one point the rangers had Cortina's cannon and had to abandon them, retaking them later. Heintzelman mentioned he and Captain Stoneman's company engaged a bandit party trying to cross into Mexico, killing six, the others escaping. In several places he said "we" did this or that, but he may have been talking about the combined force. Heintzelman did note several rangers were wounded. Other than Stoneman's participation, he does not describe or mention any action by the U.S. Army, Heintzelman, *Fifty Miles*, 155.

32. Ford, *Texas*, 275-76.

33. Ibid.

34. Ibid., 277.

35. Ibid. Heintzelman also had this opinion, *Fifty Miles*, 164.

36. RP-C. Tobin to Heintzelman, January 2, 1860.

37. Ibid., Heintzelman to Tobin, January 2, 1860. Whatever preferences he may have had, it is clear the major was willing to cooperate with whomever was in command of the rangers. Given a choice, it is also clear he would have preferred Ford.

38. Ford, *Texas*, 277.

39. Ibid.

40. Sam Houston, *The Writings of Sam Houston*, Vol. 7, edited by Amelia W. Williams and Eugene C. Barker (Austin, University of Texas Press, 1941-43) Houston to Navarro and Taylor, January 2, 1860, 395.

41. GL.Tobin to Houston, January 2, 1860.

42. Houston, *Writings*, Vol. 7, Houston to Ford, December 30, 1859, 391.

43. Ibid., Houston to Hill, December 31, 1859.

44. Ibid., 391. Houston to William C. Dalrymple, December 30, 1859.

45. Ford, *Texas*, 278.

46. GL. Taylor to Houston, January 16, 1860.

47. GL. Navarro and Taylor to Major Wm G. Tobin, January 12, 1860.

48. GL. Angel Navarro and R. H. Taylor to Gov Sam Houston, January 17, 1860.

49. RP-Rolls, John S. Ford's Company of Texas Rangers, January 20, 1860-May 17, 1860.

50. Ford, *Texas*, 280.

51. RP-Rolls, John Littleton, February 1, 1860-May 1, 1860.

52. Ford, *Texas*, 280.

53. Unless otherwise cited, the section on Bolsa Bend is based on Ford, *Texas*, 281-87.

54. RP-Rolls. Walker's Company. Woodruff died February 6, two days after being shot.

55. Ford, *Memoirs*, Vol. 4, 823.

56. RP-C. Ford to Heintzelman, Feb. 4, 1860.

57. Ford, *Memoirs*, Vol. 4, 824-25.

58. Ibid., 825-26.

59. Ford, *Texas*, 288.

60. Ibid., 288-89.

61. RP-C. Hill to Houston, February 9, 1860.

62. RP-Rolls. A.C. Hill, Texas Rangers (detachment) (Austin\Brownsville) December 30, 1859-February 1, 1860.

63. Headquarters Brownsville Expedition, Orders No. 11. February 8, 1860, quoted in Ford, *Memoirs*, Vol. 4, 826-27.

64. Ibid., Heintzelman to Joaquin Angueles, Esq., February 9, 1860.

65. Houston, *Writings*, Vol. 7, 490, Houston to Ford, February 24, 1860.

66. Ibid., 499–500, Houston to Tobin, March 5, 1860.

67. Ford's Muster Roll lists him as Daniel B. Givens, age 28.

68. Ford, *Texas*, 291.

69. Ibid., 290-95. Ford and Stoneman made a joint report, March 18, 1860, printed in "Troubles in Texas," 80 - 81.

70. Ibid., 295-98.

71. Ibid., 304-305.

72. Ibid., 299-304. Heintzelman learned of the Reynosa affair on April 6, 1860, while he was travelling with Lee. He still believed border warfare was fought according to civilized rules. His journal notation was, "What an outrage on a friendly Government!" *(Fifty Miles,* 226.)

73. Douglas Southall Freeman, *R..E. Lee*, Vol. I (New York-London: Charles Scribner & Sons, 1945), 405-409.

74. Ibid., 407.

75. Ford, *Texas*, 305.

76. Freeman, *Lee*, 408.

77. House Executive Document 81, 1st Session, 36th Congress, 2-14, published in "Troubles in Texas."

78. No. 16, Gen. Orders, Dept Texas October 30, [18]60, reprinted in Colonel M.L. Crimmins, "Colonel Robert E. Lee's Report on Indian Combats in Texas," *SHQ*, Vol. 39, No. 1 (July 1935), 21-31.

79. For example, William Addleman Ganoe, *The History of the United States Army* (New York, London: D.Appleton and Company, 1924), 242.

80. Houston, *Writings*, Vol. 7, 541-43, Houston to McKnight, March 24, 1860.

81. Heintzelman, *Fifty Miles,* 244-47; Ford, *Texas,* 303.

82. RP-Rolls, for cited units.

83. Ford, *Texas*, 308.

CHAPTER EIGHT
SAM HOUSTON AND THE INDIANS

1. Houston, *Writings*, Vol. 7, 408, Message to the Texas Legislature, January 13, 1860.

2. Ibid., 411.

3. Muster or pay rolls for thirty-two ranger units are in the State Archives. There may have been even more of these 1860-period units because not all can be traced by contemporary reports; some are known only by muster rolls. In addition, there were various volunteer detachments formed to meet a special danger.

4. Houston, *Writings*, Vol. 7, 236.

5. Ibid., 237. Earlier, on December 30, 1859, Houston had ordered Dalrymple to form a company, Houston, *Writings*, 391.

6. RP-Rolls, for companies cited.

7. Houston, *Writings*, Vol. 7, 423, Houston to Captain J. M. W. Hall, January 19, 1860.

8. RP-Rolls for cited companies.

9. Houston, *Writings*, Vol. 8, 237.

10. Houston, *Writings*, Vol. 7, 507-508, To the Chief Justices of Texas Counties, March 9, 1860.

11. Ibid., 511-12, Houston to A. G. Walker, March 10, 1860.

12. RP-C. Dixon Walker to Sam Houston, March 25, 1860.

13. RP-C. Monthly Return of Lieut Dixon Walkers Command of Mounted Rangers from Bosque County, April 1860.

14. Houston, *Writings*, Vol. 7, 238, Message to the Legislature of Texas in Extra Session.

15. Ibid., 499, Houston to Captain Peter Tumlinson, March 5, 1860.

16. RP-C, Tumlinson to Houston, April 24, 1860.

17. RP-C. Citizens of Sabinal Canyon, Uvalde, Bandera County to Governor Houston, May 30, 1860.

18. RP-C., Lampasas County to Governor Houston, June 2, 1860. Hughes was actually a lieutenant, commander of the Lampasas County Minute Men. He was in service from March 21-June 24, 1860.

19. Houston, *Writings*, Vol. 7, 496-97, Houston to Burleson, March 1, 1860.

20. RP-C. Burleson to Houston, March 13, 1860.

21. Houston, *Writings*, Vol. 7, 534-35, Proclamation Declaring an Expedition to Mexico Unauthorized, March 21, 1860.

22. Ibid., 513, Houston to John H. Conner, March 10, 1860.

23. RP-C. James S. Gillett to Governor Houston, March 14, 1860.

24. RP-C. John H. Conner to Sam Houston, Commander in Chief. Private. March 22, 1860.

25. RP-C. E. McCord to Sam Houston, April 4, 1860.

26. RP-C. John H. Conner to Sam Houston, April 19, 1860.

27. RP-Rolls. John H. Conner, January 20, 1860-May 8, 1860.

28. Houston, *Writings*, Vol. 8, 238.

29. Ibid., 239, Houston to M. T. Johnson, March 17, 1860.

30. Ibid.

31. James Pike, *The Scout and Ranger - Being the Personal Adventures of Corporal Pike* (Cincinnati & New York: J.R. Haley & Co., 1866), 83-84.

32. Judith Ann Benner, *Sul Ross - Soldier - Statesman - Educator*, (College Station: Texas A&M University Press, 1983) covers this phase of Ross' life in detail. It is of interest in a study of his entire life, but not in a survey of this nature.

33. GL. Johnson to Houston, May 30, 1860.

34. Pike, 112-13. It should be noted that some of Pike's dates do not always agree with official reports. For example, most of the rangers were back in camp by the end of July, according to Johnson.

35. RP-C. Peter F. Ross to Col. M. T. Johnson, July 28, 1860. He had been out twenty days, but his report is not quite as harrowing as Pike described—he may have put the best face on his movements. Also, it has not been generally known that Ross' Spy Company was a forty-three man Indian force. All that is usually said is he had some Tonkaway guides. See Johnson to Houston, July 30, 1860.

36. Pike, 116.

37. Ibid., 118-19.

38. GL. Johnson to Houston, July 4, 1860.

39. Houston, *Writings*, Vol. 8, 113-14, Houston to Johnson, August 4, 1860.

40. Ibid., 114-15, Houston To William C. Dalrymple and Edward Burleson, August 4, 1860.

41. Ibid., 142, Houston to Colonel M. T. Johnson, September 12, 1860.

42. Ibid., 139-40, Houston to Lawrence Sullivan Ross, September 11, 1860. RP-Rolls, L.S(ullivan) Ross, Texas Rangers, October 3, 1860-February 5, 1861.

43. RP-Rolls. L.S(ullivan) Ross, Texas Rangers, October 3, 1860-February 5, 1861.

44. The Parker "massacre" has been told many times. One of the earlier versions is in Wilbarger, 302-20.

45. Houston, Writings, Vol. 8, 215-16.

46. RP-Rolls. J.B. Barry (Lt.) January 10-February 25, 1861. Stockton was unable to form a unit.

47. Houston, *Writings*, Vol. 8, 239.

48. Ibid., 221-22.

49. See Martin W. Crimmins, "First Sergeant John W. Spangler, Company H, Second United States Cavalry," *West Texas Historical Association Yearbook*, No. 26 (Abilene, October 1950)), 68-75, for the life of Spangler.

50. This account is based on the version Ross told and wrote over a number of years, printed in 1889 by Wilbarger, 335-38. Charles Goodnight and Benjamin F. Gholson also told their stories in later years. See also, Rupert N. Richardson, "The Death of Nocona and the Recovery of Cynthia Ann Parker," *SHQ*, Vol. 46, 15-21. An early account is in the *Dallas Herald*, January 2, 1861.

51. If the Nocona arms ever reached the archives, they have long since vanished. There is no record—written or memory—of any such articles.

52. For one last-century history, see Dudley G. Wooten, *A Comprehensive History of Texas*, Vol. 2 (Dallas: William G. Scarff, 1893), 343.

53. For those interested in all sides of this question, Robert H. Williams, "The Case for Peta Nocona," Texana, Vol. 10, No. 1 (Waco: Texian Press, 1972), 55-72, explores all angles and views. His conclusion is that Ross did kill Nocona.

54. Webb, *Rangers*, 195-215.

55. Houston, *Writings*, Vol. 7, 506, Houston to John B. Floyd, March 8, 1860.

56. This time on April 14, 1860.

57. Houston, *Writings*, Vol. 8, 204-205, Houston to Floyd, November 28, 1860.

58. Webb, *Rangers*, 205. This was on February 16, 1858.

59. Some of these letters are in the Governor's Letters in the State Library. Webb, *Rangers*, quotes selected examples, 206-207. They do not conclusively prove either side of the argument and have not been reproduced here.

60. Webb, *Rangers*, 214-15.

61. Pike, 137. There is little doubt some people believed *something* was about to happen. It is likely that a scheme by the Knights of the Golden Circle, a secret organization interested in clandestine expeditions into Mexico, attracted considerable interest and support. The "plan" was a hoax and was exposed. See Heintzelman, *Fifty Miles,* 237.

62. Houston, *Writings*, Vol. 8, 127-28, Houston to Ben McCulloch, August 28, 1860.

63. Ibid.,129-30, Houston to P. T. Richardson, September 3, 1860.

64. Ibid., 240.

65. See note No. 46.

66. *Dallas Herald*, October 24, 1860.

67. Houston, *Writings*, Vol. 8, 217-18, Houston to Dalrymple, December 6, 1860,

68. Ibid., 224-25, Houston to Rogers, December 26, 1860. No muster roll exists for this company.

69. Ibid., 220-21.

70. Ibid., 225.

CHAPTER NINE

WAR AGAIN

1. Houston, *Writings*, Vol. 8, 239-40, Houston to Thomas Harrison, January 2, 1861. RP-Rolls, Thomas Harrison, Texas Mounted Rangers (Waco), January 10-June 22, 1861.

2. Houston, *Writings*, Vol. 8, 236, Message to the Legislature of Texas, in Extra session, January 21, 1861.

3. Ibid., 245.

4. RP-Rolls. William C. Dalrymple (Col), Field & Staff, Mounted Rangers, December 29, 1860-June 22, 1861.

5. GL. Ross to Houston, February 12, 1861.

6. Colonel Dalrymple's Muster Roll, note No. 4.

7. GL. Houston to Dalrymple, February 22, 1861.

8. GL. Houston to Ross, February 23, 1861.

9. RP-Rolls.G.B. Erath, McLennan County Minute Men, March 8-September 8, 1861, September 8-December 8, 1861.

10. E.W. Winkler, ed., Journal of the Secession Convention of Texas, 1861 (Austin: Austin Printing company, 1912), 384, H. A. Hammer to Allison Nelson, January 31, 1861. Hereafter JSCT.

11. This was on February 7, 1861.

12. *Dallas Herald*, March 6, 1861, quoting Ward's letter to the paper.

13. Ibid.

14. These letters and others to be noted are printed in Mildred P. Mayhall, "Camp Cooper—First Federal Fort in Texas to Fall and Events Preceeding its fall," 1861, and Events Preceeding its Fall," *Texana*, Vol. 5 (Winter 1967), 335-39.

15. Rogers' letter to the *Dallas Herald*, dated March 10, 1861, printed March 30, 1861.

16. Ibid.

17. JSCT, 271, 318, 367.

18. GL. Rogers to Houston, March 12, 1861.

19. JSCT, 383.

20. RP-Rolls. Wm. C. Dalrymple (Col) Field & Staff, Mounted Rangers, Dec 29, 1860-June 22, 1861.

21. RP-Rolls, cited commands.

BIBLIOGRAPHY

MANUSCRIPT SOURCES:

Texas State Library, Austin, Texas:

Ranger Papers:
  Correspondence, 1854-1861
  Quarter Master Records, 1850-1862
  Muster and Pay Rolls, 1846-1861
Ford, John Salmon, *Memoirs*, typescript
Governor's Letters
Houston, Sam, *Correspondence Files*, Record Group 301

The Center for American History, University of Texas at Austin:

Caperton, John, *Sketch of Colonel John C. Hays, Texas Ranger*,
  typescript

PRINTED SOURCES:

House Executive Document, No. 5, 31st Congress, 1st Session
House Executive Document, No. 52, 36th Congress, 1st Session
House Executive Document, No. 81, 36th Congress, 1st Session

ARTICLES:

Southwestern Historical Quarterly, published by the Texas State Historical
  Association of Austin, Texas:

Bender, A.B., "Opening Routes Across West Texas, Vol. 37, No. 2
  (October 1933).
Crimmins, Martin L., Colonel, "Colonel Robert E. Lee's Report on
  Indian Combats in Texas," Vol. 39, No. 1 (July 1935).
Erath, Lucy, ed., "Memoirs of George Bernard Erath," Vol. 27, No. 2
  (October 1923).
Koch, Lena Clara, "The Federal Indian Policy in Texas, 1845-1860,"
  Vol. 29, No. 3 (January 1925).
Neighbours, Kenneth F., "The Report of the Expedition of Major

Robert S. Neighbors to El Paso in 1849," Vol. 60, No. 4 (April 1957).

Richardson, Rupert N., "The Death of Nocona and the Recovery of Cynthia Ann Parker," Vol. 46, No. 1 (July 1942).

Rippy, J. Fred, "Border Troubles Along the Rio Grande," Vol. 23, No. 1 (July 1919).

Shearer, Ernest C., "The Callahan Expedition," Vol. 54, No. 4 (April 1951).

_____, "The Carvajal Disturbances," Vol. 55, No. 2 (October 1951).

West Texas Historical Association Year Book, published by the West Texas Association of Abilene, Texas:

Crimmins, Colonel Martin L., "First Sergeant John W. Spangler, Company H, Second United States Cavalry," Vol. 26 (October 1950).

Holden, W.C., "Frontier Defense During the Civil War," Vol. 4 (June 1928).

Neighbours, Kenneth F., "Indian Exodus Out of Texas in 1859," Vol. 36 (October 1960).

Texana, published by the Texian Press of Waco, Texas:

Mayhall, Mildred P., "Camp Cooper—First Federal Fort in Texas to Fall (1861) and Events Preceding its Fall," Vol. 5 (Winter 1967).

Williams, Robert H., "The Case for Peta Nocon;a," Vol. 10, No. 1 (1972).

Plum Creek Almanac, published by The Caldwell County Historical Association of Luling, Texas:

Ford, Rip, Colonel, ed., from notes made by J.S. McDowell. "Callahan's Expedition," Vol. 3, No. 2 (Fall 1985).

NEWSPAPERS:

Texas State Gazette (Austin)
Bastrop Advertiser
Dallas Herald
Galveston Daily News
Herald (San Antonio)
Zeitung (San Antonio)

BOOKS:

Barton, Henry W. *Texas Volunteers in the Mexican War*. Wichita Falls: Texian Press, 1970.

Benner, Judith Ann. *Sul Ross – Soldier – Statesman – Educator*. College Station: Texas A&M University Press, 1983.

Brown, John Henry. *Indian Wars and Pioneers of Texas*. 189?. Reprint. Austin: State House Press, 1988.

————. *History of Texas*. St. Louis: L.E. Daniel, 1893.

Chatfield, W.H., Lieut. U.S. Army. *Twin Cities of the Border*. New Orleans: E.P. Brandao, 1893.

Cortina, Juan, edited by Jerry D. Thomson. *Juan Cortina and the Texas-Mexico Frontier, 1859-1877*. El Paso: Texas Western Press, 1994.

Domenech, E. Abbe. *Missionary Adventures in Texas and Mexico*. London: Longman, Brown, Green, Longmans and Roberts, 1858.

Freeman, Douglas Southall. R.E. Lee. New York-London: Charles Scribner & Sons, 1945.

Ford, John Salmon, edited by Stephen B. Oates. *Rip Ford's Texas*. Austin: University of Texas Press, 1987.

Ganoe, Wlliam Addleman. *The History of the United States Army*. New York and London: D.Appleton and Company, 1924.

Garavaglia, Louis A. and Charles G. Worman. *Firearms of the American West*. Albuquerque: University of New Mexico Press, 1984.

Green, Rena Maverick, ed. *Samuel Maverick: Texas 1803-1870*. San Antonio: Privately printed, 1952.

Greer, James Kimmins. *Colonel Jack Hays*. New York: E.P. Dutton & Co., 1952.

Hamilton, Allen Lee. *Sentinel of the Southern Plains*. Fort Worth: Texas Christian University Press, 1988.

Heintzelman, Samuel Peter, edited by Jerry Thompson. *Fifty Miles and a Fight: Major Samuel Heintzelman's Journal of Texas and the Cortina War*. Austin: Texas State Historical Association, 1998.

Houston, Sam, edited by Amelia W. Williams and Eugene C. Barker. *The Writings of Sam Houston*. Austin: University of Texas Press, 1941-43.

Olmstead, Frederick Law. *A Journey Through Texas*. 1857. Reprint. Austin: University of Texas Press, 1989.

Pike, James. *The Scout and Ranger: Being the Personal Adventures of Corporal Pike*. Cincinnati & New York: J.R. Haley & Co., 1866.

Sowell. A.J. *Early Settlers and Indian Fighters of Southwest Texas*. 1900. Reprinted as *Texas Indian Fighters*. Austin: State House Press, 1986.

Webb, Walter Prescott. *The Texas Rangers*. Boston-New York: Houghton Mifflin Company, 1935.

Wilbarger, J.W. *Indian Depredations in Texas*. 1889. Reprint. Austin: State House Press, 1985.

Wilkins, Frederick. *The Law Comes to Texas: The Texas Rangers 1870-1901*. Austin: State House Press, 1999.

_____. *The Legend Begins: The Texas Rangers 1823-1845*. Austin: State House Press, 1996.

_____. *The Highly Irregular Irregulars, Texas Rangers in the Mexican War*. Austin: Eakin Press, 1990.

Winfrey, Dorman H. and James M. Day, editors. *The Indian Papers of Texas and the Southwest, 1825-1916*. Austin: The Pemberton Press, 1966.

Winkler, Earnest William, editor. *Journal of the Secession Convention of Texas, 1861*. Austin: Austin Printing Company, 1912.

Wooten, Dudley G. *A Comprehensive History of Texas*. Dallas: William G. Scarff, 1893.

INDEX

Nelson, G.H., 71, 72-73
New Braunfels, Tex., 50
Nickles, Robert, 87-88
Nid-el-wats (Tahuacano), 80
Nolan, Matthew, 127, 128, 130
Nueces Co., Tex., 106

Olmstead, William, 91
O'Quin (Tonkawa), 79

Palo Pinto Co., Tex., 92-93, 148
Parker Co., Tex., 148
Parker, Cynthia Ann, 148, 152ff
Parker, Isaac, 154
Parker, Quanah, 154
Paschal, George W. Jr., 85
Patton, Benjamin, 56
Pease, E.M., 43, 45-47, 49-50, 60ff, 65, 67, 75
Peta Nacona (Comanche), 148, 152-54
Piedras Negras, Mex., 52ff
Pitts, John D., 11, 61
Pitts, William A., 77, 78, 82
Placido (Tonkawa), 79
Plummer, J.B., 25, 96
Pockmark, Jim (Caddo/Anadarko), 79, 82, 83
Powers, Stephen, 105
Preston, William G., 82, 86
Pyron, William, 72

Ranchero (steamer), 121ff
Rector, Pendleton, 45-46
Reynosa, Mex., 129ff
Riddle, B., 63
Ringgold Barracks, Tex., 13, 112-13
Rio Grande City, Tex., 112ff, 117, 119, 132
Roberts, Jacob, 15
Rogers, E.W., 157-58, 162-63, 165
Rollins (agent), 35
Roma, Tex., 113ff
Ross, Lawrence S. "Sul," 91, 144-45, 147ff, 155, 157, 158, 159, 160-61
Ross, Peter F., 145-46
Ross, Shapley P., 15, 78, 79ff, 91, 97
Rountree, Volney, 32
Runnels, H.R., 70, 75ff, 78-79, 87, 93, 96, 98, 101, 104, 110, 135

Sabinal, Tex., 140
San Antonio, Tex., 2, 5, 6, 11, 12, 40, 45, 61, 105, 161
San Marcos, Tex., 57
San Patricio, Tex,. 28
San Saba, Tex., 68, 79
Sansom, John W., 65
Santa Fe, N.Mex., 2
Scott, Winfield, 22-23
Searcy, Oliver, 87-88

Seguin, Tex., 51, 63-64, 105
Seminole Indians, 12, 34-35
Shaw, Jim, 6, 80
Shaw, Owen, 40-42
Smith, Augustus, 56
Smith, J.M., 15, 144-45
Smith, James, 96
Smith, Persifor F., 43, 46, 47, 49-50, 57, 60-61
Smith, Samuel G., 56
Smith, W.F., 8
Smock, 11
Sommerville, M.W., 151
Spangler, John W., 149-50
Spence, Jack, 33
Steele, David, 15, 26
Steiner, J.M., 96
Stephenville, Tex., 140
Stevens, Ed, 29-30
Stockton, Thomas, 148, 157
Stoneman, George, 109, 112, 115, 121, 125, 127, 128-29, 130
Sublett, David L., 163, 164, 165
Sullivan, Doc, 15, 28-29
Sutton, John S., 15
Sutton, R.E., 10, 11

Tackett, Rev., 80
Tankersley, James H., 82, 86
Tarrant Co., Tex., 139, 144
Taylor, Charles, 47
Taylor, Robert H., 118-20
Texas Mounted Volunteers, Cos. A-F, 43-44
Thomas, George H., 98
Thompson, W.B., 104
Tijerina, Miguel, 102, 103
Tobin, G.W., 45
Tobin, William G., 65, 104ff, 108, 111, 112, 114-16, 117-18, 119, 121, 123, 127, 138
Todd, Dr., 142-43
Tom, Alf, 33
Tom, Hughes, 55
Tom, William, 65
Travis, C.E., 43
Treviño, Andres, 132
Treviño, Juan, 131
Tumlinson, Peter, 109, 111, 112, 115, 116, 117, 121, 123, 140-41
Twiggs, David E., 161

Van Dorn, Earl, 78, 91, 94
Victoria Co., Tex., 110

Waco, Tex., 144
Walker, Andrew J., 13-14, 29-30, 31-32, 35, 38
Walker, Dixon, 139, 140
Walker, Joseph, 111, 112, 116, 117-18